I AM THE MARKET

I AM THE MARKET

How to Smuggle Cocaine
by the Ton, in Five Easy Lessons

LUCA RASTELLO

Translated from the Italian by Jonathan Hunt

FABER AND FABER, INC.
An affiliate of Farrar, Straus and Giroux   New York

FABER AND FABER, INC.

An affiliate of Farrar, Straus and Giroux

18 West 18th Street, New York 10011

Originally published in 2009 by Chiarelettere editore srl—Gruppo Editoriale
Mauri Spagnol S.p.A., Italy, as *Io sono il mercato: Come trasportare cocaina a
tonnellate e vivere felici*
English translation originally published, in slightly different form, in 2010 by
Granta Books, Great Britain, as *I Am the Market: How to Smuggle Cocaine by the
Ton and Live Happily*
Published in the United States by Faber and Faber, Inc.
First American edition, 2011

Library of Congress Cataloging-in-Publication Data
Rastello, Luca, 1961–
  [Io sono il mercato. English]
  I am the market : how to smuggle cocaine by the ton, in five easy lessons /
Luca Rastello ; translated from the Italian by Jonathan Hunt.
      p. cm.
  "Originally published in 2009 by Chiarelettere editore srl Gruppo
Editoriale Mauri Spagnol S.p.A., Italy, as Io sono il mercato: Come trasportare
cocaina a tonnellate e vivere felici."
  ISBN 978-0-86547-949-4 (alk. paper)
  1. Cocaine industry.   2. Drug traffic.   3. Drug dealers.   I. Hunt,
Jonathan, 1951–   II. Title.

HV5810 .R3713 2011
363.45—dc22

                                                                2010033104

Designed by Abby Kagan

www.fsgbooks.com

10 9 8 7 6 5 4 3 2 1

Look at me. I am the market. I am the world as it is.

By the end, if you've followed me attentively, you'll be able to set up in business yourself.

But before I begin, I'll tell you a story.

Contents

I AM THE MARKET

Prologue with Theologian

This story ends at Maiquetía International Airport in Caracas. Father Antonio lives in a run-down barrio of the capital. His parish church consists of four posts, a few rough wooden planks, and a corrugated-iron roof. His congregation is desperately poor. Father Antonio himself can barely make ends meet. But—unfortunately for him—he's a man of learning, a theologian. A guy who during nights of anguish thinks, I've been here for six years, and I keep Our Lord in a fruit crate wrapped in a bit of tinfoil. Okay: God has no home, and His home is everywhere, but poor Father Antonio thought at least a little beauty was necessary to pay Him homage. He thought goodness included beauty. Though it's true, he said to himself, that even poverty can be sublimated into absolute beauty.

Being a man of learning, Father Antonio was invited one day to a conference in Bogotá, a big meeting that involved three afternoons of spiritual exercises. Of course, he didn't have a penny for the journey and had to cadge funds from the curia, a parsimonious institution if ever there was one. At Bogotá airport, despite his limited finances, Father Antonio looked for a taxi to take him to the city center, but the taxis were all full to bursting, with people hanging on to the doors. That's how they do things in those parts. So here is our Father, standing like a *panettone* in the square outside arrivals. A *panettone* in a cassock attracts attention, so a man steps forward and offers him a lift. Father Antonio accepts, probably because he doesn't know what's going through his benefactor's head. Something like: There's a priest sitting beside me. Who's going to stop me? Of course, the hood of the man's car is stashed full of cocaine, and when he sees the priest looking lost, he seizes his chance. The streets of Bogotá are clogged with traffic; there's time to make friends and chat. The two of them hit it off. The man listens, shows an interest, and Father Antonio tells him about the barrio, the church, the hunger, the loose soil of the hillside, which at the first drops of rain starts sliding down the slope, taking his parishioners' shacks with it.

"When are you flying back to Caracas, Father?"

"In three days' time."

"Here's my number. Call me. I'll take you to the airport."

Excellent, thinks the priest: three days of spiritual exercises and two lifts—plus a small donation at the end of it, I shouldn't wonder. Not a bad profit for someone whose pockets are empty except for a promissory note from the episcopal secretariat. But the donation, when it comes, is far from small, at least by the standards of a suburban priest. At the boarding gate on the journey home, a cool five thousand dollars are slipped into his hand. The priest can't believe his eyes; he has visions of a floor for his church, a nice big slab of cement, with foundations and everything, and for a few years at least he won't have to worry about the church slithering down the hillside along with the mud. Of course, the Colombian's money runs out immediately, but Father Antonio has kept his benefactor's phone number. He calls him, thanks him, and asks . . .

Again the man astonishes him: "I'll come to Caracas, Father. I'll see you there."

He's certainly a very pious person.

The priest shows him the slab of cement, explains his plans, makes it clear that he needs help. The man pretends to think about it; in fact he's already done his thinking. "I can help you, Father. But my help might offend your conscience." His manner has become more confidential. "I can't give you money. But I can give you something better. Cocaine. The best there is. I'll give it to you free of charge!"

Naturally, the friar is horrified at first, but the temptation is as great as the scruples of his conscience. He's surrounded by sickness, hunger, violence, something approaching chaos. A theologian's analogy occurs to him: How was St. Peter's built in Rome? With money that flowed from the alms box and souls rising blessed to heaven? No. He knows that the great works of Renaissance art are caked in the blood of the poor. The same poor who suffer all around him in the mud of the barrio. And yet the Roman basilica still stands. And it's an example to the world. More: a comfort, a refuge for those same people who carried its weight on their shoulders—the destitute. It's the very symbol of Christianity, the most revolutionary message the world has seen, carved for all time in the colonnade, in the domes, in the great altars. Father Antonio doesn't want to build a basilica; he's not after works of art. All he wants is a decent church. Besides, he knows only too well that many of his flock already buy cocaine on the streets, and God knows what filth it's cut with. Keeping an eye on his people like this might be a good thing. A way of limiting the damage.

I could give it to them myself. And I'd put the money they paid me into the alms box so that it could be used for their own benefit. The church would be there to remind them of the path of righteousness; their health would benefit, and so would their souls. What difference is there, in the end, between my money and that of Leo X?

It may seem absurd, but the priest was right. And the dealer from Bogotá really was a pious man. And he really did supply him with the best cocaine in the world: the pearl.

The pearl. They call it that because if you put it on the palm of your hand, it takes on an almost oily consistency, with a hint of iridescent color. A beautiful sight! There are very few people who can afford stuff like that. No more than a few dozen in the whole world. The big producers don't make it—only small, self-employed farmers. It's produced in limited quantities; it requires mature, old leaves, not the newly sprouted leaflets that are gathered in the big harvests and are pale green. So making the pearl takes time; you have to accept a less intensive exploitation of the plant, settle for only one harvest a year instead of three. And the shrub that produces the leaf is a self-seeding plant. If you lose it, it's not easy to sow again. Its leaves are larger than those of nursery plants, so they're easily seen from above. It grows only at high altitudes, where there's less oxygen. You can't plant it in rows unless you want to be bombed with North American defoliants. So it sprouts only on small allotments. It has to be dried in the sun, not in a microwave, and not once, but twice—first as a leaf and then as coca paste. The paste is pressed by hand, as it was in the old days, not with a filter press meant for drying kaolin, which all large-scale producers use nowadays.

The pearl is incompatible with haste. And haste is the curse of the big-time narco. Everything immediately, and payment in cash, *al brinco rabioso*, as they say in South America. So, whole-sale maceration in big plastic-lined pits? Hydrochloric acid, ether to increase the volatility of the impurities, various acids to extract the alkaloid, cutting, and drying in a microwave oven? No, the pearl is made by hand, with the help of the sun, and packaged using pure, edible oil. Top-quality lime to catalyze the alkaloid and produce oxygen. Then the lime has to be removed. The standard way of doing that is with hydrochloric acid and ammonia, a quick method that confers a yellow color and burns away part of the active ingredient. But the pearl is treated only with acetone and ether. Acetone burns away only what needs to be burned away, the impurities; it does so in a natural way and imparts a pinkish color. The ether evaporates, giving it that pearly tinge, and the substance reduces. When the lime precipitates, everything happens in the paste. Only 6 or 7 percent of the original substance remains. At this point the process has to be repeated with the patience of an old al-chemist. So the paste is boiled, left to macerate for three days, and, finally, dried again. In the sun, of course. You've spent at least ten days on processing alone since the time of harvesting, compared with the three it takes in large-scale production. You've produced all the smells in the world, and so, unless your farm is in a very secluded location, you've put yourself in grave danger: you've allowed some highly toxic vapors to escape, pre-serving only the best of the substance. You've also run the risk of "black work." In manual production the substance is more likely to be burned by the acids and turn black and as hard as stone. If that should happen, you're ruined. You've wasted your harvest. All you can do with the black substance is make crack or freebase, to be inhaled with a towel over your head, like when you have a cold: lethal stuff, fit only for the blacks of Los Angeles or the Haitians, who mix it with tar and roll it into balls. Rotgut, only 30 to 50 percent pure at most, recycled garbage that nobody wants on the wholesale market. Whereas the pearl is a marvel, 96 percent pure, minimum. But producing it involves a cost, a risk, and a sacrifice. It has to be well remunerated. For example, there's a small farmer who produces it in the Sierra Guajira. Wonderful stuff. It costs an arm and a leg, but he never makes more than three kilos a year for fear of flooding the market and impairing quality in the interests of quantity and processing speed. It's the "slow food" of the jungle.

Father Antonio can't stop thinking: This cocaine, instead of going around the world brutalizing it and unleashing evil, would be a redeeming sacrifice. It would help the poor, make the sick feel less unhappy, force the parishioners to stay close to their good shepherd. A real vegetable Lamb of God. The narco too is enthusiastic. I'm not giving you faith, my friend, he thinks, but I'm giving you something that can help faith. And I'm giving you the chance for a decent life for you and your godforsaken district. With a deal like this, a little place in heaven might even be found for the trafficker himself.

The priest's mind is racked with doubts, but in the end the benefits far outweigh the costs. What's more, the Franciscan— of course he's a Franciscan, the order of logicians par excellence—has had the crucial epiphany, the one that makes it all possible: he won't distribute the cocaine, he won't send it out onto the streets to do harm. He'll have it consumed in the parish church, under supervision. A sacred shooting gallery. And an exclusive one, at that. The finest drugs ever produced by man will be consumed there, in conditions of absolute safety. As for the transportation, he'll look after that himself. He doesn't want his flock involved in any shady business. After all, the money for the journeys is no longer a problem, the local church has been founded and is solid, the community is prospering—heaven on earth, almost. It seems you don't even have to die to reach the Lord anymore. Father Antonio flies to Bogotá now and then; he's had a cassock made with a special seam around the edges and a thick lining; he packs the stuff into small oblong bags that he sews into the garment. Everything seems to be going smoothly. No cop would dare let his mutt sniff a sacred robe, and besides, Father Antonio is a well-known figure at the airport by now. Everyone knows he's a keen participant in spiritual exercises all over the continent.

Machines, though—they don't have souls. Least of all stupid machines like escalators, primitive contraptions that you can find in any Third World store. Or airport. Cheap belts of metal, made from sheets just as flimsy as those that covered Father Antonio's old parish church. Ill-interlocking pieces of tin, capable of snagging the edge of a long clerical robe, tugging at it, hauling its unfortunate wearer to the ground, ripping it, holing it, spilling out all that gorgeous stuff and scattering it, white as the purest of pearls, dazzling as the Caribbean sun, all over the airport hall.

At his trial Father Antonio was found guilty. There was really no getting around it. The accident had happened in front of everyone, hundreds of eyes had seen it, and the newspapers and TV had jumped on the story. But they made sure he spent as little time as possible in jail. After all, there's a judge in Caracas. And he too is a pious man, capable of understanding the profound reasons for what has occurred. So the friar is locked up in prison and then, very quietly, let straight out again. There are dozens of witness statements in his favor. He offered only consumption; there was no selling. Father Antonio wasn't a dealer. He wasn't in competition with those who sell retail, nor with those who sell wholesale. At worst he was in competition with One who sells heaven at prices far higher than his— corporeal death, for example. But these are problems that a good Franciscan theologian knows how to grapple with.

Introduction

What is offered here is an exercise. Its subject is cocaine, a substance that decides a far greater part of our lives than we are disposed to think. Even—perhaps especially—if we don't use it.

Cocaine. A sea of cocaine.

The newspapers like talking about it. It always makes for good copy: stories of gangland shoot-outs in the narrow streets of some Mediterranean city, colorful portraits of dealers great and small, the occasional alarmed—and cliché-ridden—reportage on the increase in consumption, especially among the young, in discos and nightclubs. Or chemical analysis of the water of a river near a big city, which reveals such quantities of dissolved cocaine in the sewers as to suggest prodigious everyday use. Cocaine by the ton. And news in equal measure.

Sometimes one comes across less fascinating information, which is difficult to work up into a crime story. It speaks of money. Of entire national economies—and not those of small, underdeveloped countries—kept afloat by the money from co-caine smuggling. For example, the ten billion dollars that the Colombian cartels invest every year in the financial system of Florida (the fourth most populous state in the United States, crucial to the election of George Bush in 2000). Without that sum the collapse of the entire local banking system would be inevitable, with consequences and repercussions on a global scale. According to the 1999 report of the Mexican Center for Investigation and National Security, "if drug smuggling were to be eradicated, the economy of the United States would suffer losses of between 19 and 22 percent, while the Mexican economy would see a fall of 63 percent."

It is as well to remember that as far as the drug cartels are concerned, there are no nation-states, no borders. We're talking about markets that are capable of influencing the world economy and therefore of determining how questions of sovereignty, the entitlement to and exercise of rights, and international relations are decided.

On the face of it, this enormous, menacing, submerged world is being attacked with maximum zeal by powerful political forces. For example, the colossal antidrug apparatus set up by George Bush, Sr., and dramatized as the War on Drugs, an elephantine enterprise that involved military control of the South American continent, agreements with governments, and the massive deployment of high-tech equipment for aerial surveillance and for spraying defoliants on the coca crops. An enterprise that in 2000 put a burden of 103 billion dollars on U.S. public expenditure, a sum comparable to the gross domestic product of a country like Portugal. But the enterprise failed in its aims from the outset. In 1992 a report by the American House of Representatives set out the reasons for its defeat: "In 1984," it says, "coca leaf was grown only in Peru, Bolivia,

Colombia and Ecuador. Today it is grown in many other countries, refined in 9, transported across 25 and consumed in at least 18 Latin-American nations." To leave no doubt about the matter, the report concludes, "This expansion has been caused by the United States government and its policy of repression." Whenever the War on Drugs has concentrated on one region, the drug lords have reacted by moving the plantations and the markets, and the result has been a widening of the areas of production. The cartels have been very imaginative, setting up, in the golden age of drug smuggling, an endless succession of improvised landing strips for their planes on hundreds of atolls, and even, at one point (during the years of Pablo Escobar, the greatest drug smuggler of all time), digging an extraordinary tunnel under the border between Mexico and the United States. This is the most closely guarded border in the world (aboveground at least), ending in the formidable "Tijuana barrier," a monumental fence built to prevent illegal immigration, which runs for fourteen miles, right into the waters of the ocean.

Besides, there is a widespread belief among the drug lords, as we shall see, that the transnational strategies for combating their operations are nothing but propaganda, masking a substantial connivance: the economy of the criminal market is so indispensable to the legal economy that the result is a universal policy of live and let live, behind a facade of repression. The drug lords see the War on Drugs as a big show that has been played out to their advantage. According to the legend of Don Pablo Escobar, as handed down by his hangers-on, admirers, and beneficiaries, what brought about the collapse of the Medellín cartel, which he founded, was his decision to move into the world of politics instead of negotiating a form of subterranean coexistence that could guarantee the economic futures of both the drug dealers and the no less massive empire of antinarcotics bodies (national and supranational police agencies, institutions, research centers, and universities, as well as the public and especially the private rehabilitation communities). Two colossal industries that need each other if they are to survive.

The more than 100 billion dollars spent on the military repression of the drug plantations contrasts with the paltry sum invested in reducing demand (10 million dollars) and the miserly 4.5 million dollars invested in plans for replacing illegal crops. The aim of these plans is to induce the growers of coca and opium poppy to sow their land with less harmful products such as cacao, coffee, and rice, or to turn their fields into pastureland. The results of this strategy have been disastrous. Poor regions are forced to grow crops that are unsuited to the local climate or are not competitive internationally. The consequences for the growers are starvation and a headlong rush into the arms of the drug smugglers, the only people who can offer them any prospect of survival.

Drug plantations are spreading everywhere in the countries affected by the plans for alternative crop development promoted by the U.S. government or the United Nations. There are many paradoxical cases: in the Ivory Coast, for example, the cultivation of rice was supported by the International Monetary Fund in the early 1990s through the building of colossal dams, but the maintenance costs of the dams proved so burdensome that it was impossible for the Ivorians to compete with rice produced in Thailand, which was itself receiving financial support from the IMF. Result: over the past decade the Ivory Coast has climbed steadily up the league table of the leading world producers of marijuana. No less disastrous is the widespread use of herbicides sprayed by American planes on forests all over

South America, mainly destroying the tiny allotments of the campesinos. Today the drug smugglers active in South America control a territory ten times the size of the one they controlled before the defoliation campaigns.

The incredibly high profitability of illegal drugs makes them the fastest instrument of enrichment in the world, and one that has been fundamental in determining the outcomes of wars. For example, during the conflict in the former Yugoslavia, three-way drugs-for-arms deals allowed the international embargoes to be circumvented. Drug trafficking has also given new tools of domination to the ruthless politico-commercial elites that came to power in so many parts of the world after the collapse of the bipolar U.S.A.-U.S.S.R. order.

But why have commodities like cocaine (or the opium poppy, so crucial today to the destinies of central Asia, overwhelmed by the war in Afghanistan, and of the entire West) become the mainstays of the world economy? An investment of one dollar in the production of cocaine gives a return of a thousand dollars at the other end of the distribution chain. Never in human history has there been such a profitable commodity. What confers such power on a form of agricultural production that is in other respects comparable to others? The answer is as simple as it is embarrassing: the artificial difficulty of access to the market at the retail level. In a word, prohibition.

Contrary to what may be thought, the producing countries suffer from this profitability and the rich countries benefit from it. With the fall of protectionist barriers and the local economies' new exposure to global competition, it is inevitable that for the poorer agricultures, the only competitive raw materials will be drugs. In that part of the world once called "the South," there is a tendency to regard drugs as legal merchandise, and this is not a view that is easy to challenge if one considers that most of the profits from this trade go not to the producers but, as in Florida, straight into the banks of the rich countries, those shrines to legality. The farmers receive only 0.5 percent of the wealth created by selling the merchandise in the West, and there is no cheaper way of paying off the foreign debt than with the remainder of that wealth. The "North"—if it can still be called that in these times of globalization—engaged as it is in the War on Drugs, seems to judge these substances according to a dual morality: tools of the devil when they undermine the health of its young, manna from heaven when the capital they generate fills the vaults of its banks.

What control can democratic countries exercise over a market chiefly dominated by the criminal economy? What can be said about the wars that bloody the planet if we are not prepared to acknowledge the extent to which they have been caused by intertwined interests and individuals that have evaded scrutiny until very recently?

To put it crudely, when we talk about drugs, and the economy connected with drugs, we are not talking about only one part of the planet. What is offered here is not a view of the criminal world but a criminal view of the world.

And yet the stories of cocaine, at least those that we read in the newspapers or see on television, tend to suggest that the movement of one of the most profitable substances in the history of humanity takes place by means of a system of couriers who conceal the merchandise in the false bottoms of suitcases or swallow it after sealing it in special ovules resistant to the gastric juices. How much cocaine can be carried from one continent to another using these methods? A few kilos? A few hundred kilos? But the sea of white powder that is submerging Europe and changing its destiny cannot be transported in overnight bags, artificial limbs, or gastro-protected capsules: sustaining the market—even just the European market—requires tons of pure cocaine, which must then be broken down into profitable fixes for the retail market.

Tons. Which means ships, cargo planes, containers—large, cumbersome, extremely tangible amounts. Curiously, no one has ever explained how it is possible to get all that merchandise through harbors and airports equipped with the most sophisticated means of detection. Much less how customs offices are deceived, legal and fiscal checks eluded, and documents prepared to disguise a mountain of white powder. There is no shortage of analyses and data, just as there is no shortage of biographies of great criminals. And yet we still lack the true story of a world about which we know very little: its practices, sensibilities, and values, its vision of the world. It may be useful, for once, to suspend all moral judgment, forget all the clichés, and try to see the world through the eyes of someone who lives and builds his fortune in the shadowy zone of the drug cartels.

The work that lay behind this book consisted of an attempt (a hazardous one, in all honesty) to allow these "shadowy individuals" to hold the floor, without censoring them—simply to listen as they told their stories and described their methods. Such an approach can enable us to look into the eyes of this *monstrum* (literally, "prodigy, object of wonder") that is so fascinating and yet so rarely talked about. Discovering how a ton of cocaine is hidden and how customs controls are evaded, learning how the colossal empire we loosely call "drug smuggling" has reorganized and how it interacts with the rival, "good" empire is a surprisingly enlightening experience. It can change the way we look at everyday life and some of our most common assumptions. We may never look at the car we drive, the wire that brings electricity into our home, or the computer that a benefactor donates to a nonprofit institution in the same way again.

The stories told in the book are all absolutely true, but it should be borne in mind on every page that the voice is that of the criminal participant. The style, the sensibility, the choice of images, and the commentary are all his, as are the linguistic and mental habits and the anomalous morality that governs the narrative. The reader will not be surprised if the narrator prefers to remain anonymous. The insights he provides carry risks, and not only in the legal sphere.

These stories concern one of the most radical changes in the world economy, and they provide a context for reflecting on the contemporary world in a new and unusual way, but they are also stories of people, of questionable tastes, of risks and adventures. They have been collected in the conviction that a handbook on drug smuggling, in narrative form, can provide some defense against the enormous power of drug smuggling itself. One of the devil's most cunning ruses, they say, is to have convinced mortals of his nonexistence. Or of his total otherness.

LESSON ONE: The Problem

Finding a Better Solution Than Bribery

The secret of all secrets is the darkness, and you're here to discover it. It's the masterstroke, the brain wave, the revolution. The method of delivery in the dark changed the system of drug smuggling, changed the economy, changed the world. It's a simple idea, as all the best ideas are, but one with unpredictable consequences: moving drugs by the ton using the legal economy as your carrier. If you are to understand it and put it into practice, there are a few little-known facts that you need to be aware of.

Have you seen *Pulp Fiction?* The War on Drugs was at its height when the film came out, and Tarantino had grasped something that Bush's strategists hadn't. The international market was changing; the American market was in deep crisis. Ronald Reagan's smile had been extinguished, euphoria had drowned on a Black Friday that burst the financial bubble of the 1980s, the age of obligatory success and yuppie extravagance was over, and legions of forty-somethings had been knocked off the ladder to easy riches. Many people north of Tijuana began to taste the bitter fruits of failure. We traffickers too were attentive to the changes in demand, of course: some studied trends in consumption, as people do in all other businesses, and only an imbecile could still think of selling stimulants to the same poor bastards dressed in jacket and tie who had been our customers the year before. More relaxed models were needed now in the less "triumphant" United States. It was time to diversify supply, to suggest alternatives—sedative ones, if possible. And look what comes up on the screen. Instead of the hair-gelled, cocaine-snorting killers who abounded in the films of earlier years, here are Samuel L. Jackson and John Travolta, with their tailored suits and their professional calm, pulling out syringe and tourniquet like any junkies in Naples or Marseille.

Yes, some relatively new substances emerge during that period, such as ecstasy-like synthetic drugs (though in fact the Germans had already used those in the First World War), and old hallucinogenic classics such as LSD come back into fashion, but what the mass of North American consumers are really asking us for is good old heroin, the queen of sedatives. In the 1990s the supply of heroin in America rises by 300 percent, from the ghettos of the Southwest to the middle-class districts in the big cities. Naturally, production too falls into line. It's expensive to transport heroin from Asia, and the land is fertile over here too, so in Bolivia, Colombia, Guatemala, Peru, and above all in Mexico, a new plant springs up all over the place: *amapola*, the opium poppy.

A lot of things change: long-established organizations that used to control the routes and the refinement lose influence;

even the Italians don't matter as much anymore. It's the Mexicans now who supply the United States with heroin and who have largely supplanted the old godfathers.

And cocaine? It has to find other markets or risk overproduction and all the other problems that any shrewd trader associates with a big warehouse full of unsold merchandise. Europe, then, but it's not an easy market. It's accustomed to thinking of cocaine as a luxury product, fuel for the rich when they need to boost their performance. A niche market, shall we say? At the beginning of the last decade, flooding it with mass supply becomes a matter of survival. We need to take unprecedented quantities across the Atlantic, think up new strategies. The system needs new perspectives, new rules, a new professionalism. This is where the people known in the trade as "*sistemistas*" come in: they're the heart of wholesale smuggling, formidable logistic experts capable of shifting goods in tons, evading the nets of the police and the traps and snares that catch out every good entrepreneur. The *sistemistas*—that's us.

The market is changing, it's adapting to the global transformations, but it's huge, and it still offers great opportunities to anyone who knows what he's doing. The possibilities are almost infinite. Let's get to work, then.

The War Between the Cartels

The problem was bribery. Around 1986, five hundred kilos produced in the forest by the Cali cartel in Colombia and carried by truck to the port of Buenaventura required significant investment. In the first place, you had to have the truck drivers on your payroll. But in the harbor too, dozens of customs officers had to be paid not to ask questions. The merchandise might have to be loaded, for example, as it often was in those days, onto a coffee container—"longboats," we used to call them—and taken to Los Angeles or San Diego. Back then we didn't worry too much about protecting the shipments, and nobody thought seriously about substances for putting the dogs off the scent or opacifiers to fool the densitometers; it wasn't particularly important to hide the merchandise well. You put it in the sacks of coffee, and that was it. There was no need to do any more than that because in both Los Angeles and San Diego you had your own people in the harbor, not least the police, dogs included. Didn't you know? Most of the breeding kennels for sniffer dogs in the Caribbean were run by us. Amusing, eh? And of course, we were only too happy to give the police our best animals free of charge. We gave them the dogs that were supposed to intercept our merchandise.

That's the way of the world.

Cops, then, but also shipping agents, carriers, and customs officers, just like in the port of departure. These guys were Yankees, though—lieutenants and captains on contracts. The blue-clad cops of the United States are expensive, far more so than a Colombian *cholo*, even those with stripes on their sleeves and braid on their chest. And don't forget the middle part of the journey, between Buenaventura and San Diego—the ship's captain, the radio operators, and the crew. An enormous number of people who all need to be bribed. And the point is this: if they've taken bribes from you, they might take them from others. From anyone. In other words, you never know how far you can trust them.

Too many expenses. And too many men involved, all of them liable to rat on you sooner or later. The most important thing for a good narco to know is the most banal thing of all, the thing you're in danger of forgetting when you're faced with a beautiful sunset, a generous gesture, or an evening with a woman: every man has his price.

The bosses of the cartels who warred against one another about twenty years ago were only too mindful of this law. In every port it's easy to find a little fish who'll be ready to reveal a lot if a policeman looking for promotion grabs him by the balls. And all it takes for a policeman to grab the right little fish by the balls is a tip-off. That's the way to deal with your competitors. The result in the late 1980s and early 1990s was the collapse of billion-dollar operations, massive losses of merchandise, money, and good men who ended up behind bars or, worse, being protected in some federal witness program.

There were no alternatives at the time. From the banana-boat sailor to the shipping agent—and maybe even the ordinary down-and-out guys sitting around day and night on the benches of ports or in the waiting rooms of airports—you had to give everybody something. And with the ruthless competition that had developed, you can see why handling heavy loads had become a serious problem. The cunningly altered suitcase, the swallowed ovules, yes, of course, you could always get those through, but—I ask again—how much can you transport using those methods? And the trouble was that the war between the cartels was reaching its height just as a huge market was opening up in Europe.

Cocaine Invades Europe

The first to wake up were the Croats. They'd known for some time that there was going to be a war, and if there's one thing you can always be sure of, it's that a war means there is lots of money to be made. The Serbs controlled the supply route of

Turkish heroin and took their slice from all the westward shipments, and the Croats, who wanted to break away from the old
Yugoslavia, started to seize everything that passed through their
territory. Listen to this, it's incredible. In 1990 the Croats were
rewarded by Interpol for having the most efficient police force
in the world when it came to seizing heroin. Then in 1991, all
of a sudden, the most efficient police in the world were no
longer seizing a gram. Simple: they had set up in business.
They were an independent state now, and they took their
bribes too, just as the Belgrade officials did. At that point
heroin had to find a new route. The Serbs didn't want to lose
the largest share of the business, and heroin stopped passing
through Croatia.

But there was us. Well, not me, actually. I don't like working
with the Slavs—they're ruthless, they kill just to show off their
muscles, they have a completely different mentality from the
South Americans. You see, the old Croat Nazis who fled the
country after the Second World War had made their fortunes
in South America on the back of the financial transactions
connected with cocaine; and on the eve of a nationalist war
(something a good Nazi is always hankering after) they had an
opportunity to combine what was useful (business) with pleasure (arming their fatherland). They were in contact with people of the caliber of the Fidanzatis and, for money laundering,
the Caruana-Cuntreras in the Antilles, down on Aruba—in
other words with Cosa Nostra. And Cosa Nostra had some able
people on the border of the new Croatia. One of them became
famous—Felicetto Maniero, I'm sure you remember him . . .
The Brenta Mafia, they called it. It was Cosa Nostra plus
the Croats. Colossal trails of cocaine led from the Andean
cordilleras all the way to Zagreb, where in the meantime the ex-
Nazis of Herzegovina (mountain Croats, as ferocious as moun-

tain goats, grouped together into family clans more tightly knit than those of the Calabrians and therefore very well suited to our line of business) had gained control of several ministries, notably the most profitable of all at the time, the Ministry of Defense, which was run by our man Gojko Šušak, a guy who only one year earlier had been running a pizzeria in Montreal. They needed to get the stuff circulating; there was national independence and at least a couple of wars to be paid for. And besides, the stuff needed to find a new market because of the decline of consumption in the United States. It was time to change gear. El Dorado was in Europe now.

That's how it works: when private and public interests miraculously coincide, the result is revolution. That, for us, was the revolution.

I've never been sure whether I really like the Italians. Oh, I don't mean the organizations! Everybody's learned from them. Where I come from, everybody remembers people like old Sam Giancana, who was one of the fathers of the United States in a sense, though they're never going to put his big nose on Mount Rushmore. And his successors too—less brash, smoother guys, the fathers of governors. You can learn something from them at every turn, every time they breathe, from every gesture they make. If you're not completely stupid, that is. But in Italy there's an almost innate predilection for monopoly, for coming to a private understanding with people you like on favorable terms; it's rare to find an Italian who has a clear idea of the real meaning of free trade. And that's fine—I don't say it isn't. But to my way of thinking, a man's profession comes first. The Italians are brilliant at setting up a family and making it function. But it's the technique that I'm talking about. The logistics. It's not the families that do the work. They put up the money, open the markets, control the outlets with their military machines, but then, for the more technical parts of the job, they turn to professionals who are able to solve real problems. They need people who are reliable, creative, practical, and able to save their clients time and money. There aren't many people like that, believe me, and that's why the opportunities are great. People like us don't grow in a family; we're entrepreneurs, independent minds. For the important operations you need unpredictability and organization, the ability to plan and also to improvise. We're no different from the best business managers, only a bit better because of the additional difficulties we have to cope with.

So forget the ideas you've got from watching films. If you've bought a barrel of hair gel and a pinstripe suit, you can throw them away. What is a drug smuggler, technically speaking? A service provider. Nothing else. It doesn't matter if the clients are heads of state, soldiers, guerrillas, mafiosi, or politicians. They're at either end of the distribution chain. At one end they produce, at the other they sell and reap the profits of the move from wholesale to retail. They don't smuggle: too dangerous, too difficult. In the middle of the chain there's no room for families, honor, guns, and the sound tracks of Ennio Morricone. It's a question of organizational science. Here, with me, you learn technical concepts; for the myth, apply at the other window.

I'll explain the whole thing. But you must be patient and keep your ears pinned back. You must always think that if everything goes well, at the end you'll really be able to enjoy yourself. But in order to get there, you have to be able to crush the competition: guns and threats don't keep you in business; customers don't choose you out of fear or affinity. They choose you for your efficiency. In order to keep going for a long time, you have to get to a point where you select your own customers. You get to choose between the Communist caudillo, the nostalgic mafioso, and the Contra operatives in Washington—they don't choose you. Once you've achieved that, you've arrived. There are many people out there who would like to decide on your behalf and know very well how to make you toe the line, if it suits them. So it's a matter of earning people's respect. I succeeded in doing that. I built up a credit of two million dollars in cocaine. I mean that at the height of my career I could lose a consignment worth two million without paying for it, either with my wallet or with my life. Because they trusted me, I worked for the Orejuelas in Cali, for Castro, and Tirofijo. For many years I was the only person operating at that level. Because I solved the cartels' biggest problem—I invented the trick of tricks: delivery in the dark. I was one of the guys who opened up the South Road. It was just after the fall of the empire of Pablo Escobar. Don Pablo will go down in history for devising and popularizing the multi-operator method taken up by our industry. He was intelligent, and he was the first to see that the bribery-based system was a problem, and he tried to replace it with one of his inventions. He was a guy who thought big. As big as the tunnel.

Don Pablo Escobar and the Horizontal Elevator

He was no pussycat, it's true. But he was a jovial, lively, brilliant guy, and sincerely concerned about his people. At least so everyone thought at the time of his success. He had that rather molelike, amiable face, the black eyes behind which you sensed an intelligence constantly at work, curls thinning on his temples, dark mustachios. You know who he looked like? Gianni Minà, the journalist famous for his fawning interviews with Fidel Castro. I swear it. At the time, Don Pablo was still on the crest of the wave, he hadn't yet annoyed the political establishment to the extent of getting himself assassinated, and he enjoyed a freedom that perhaps no narco has had since. In effect it was he, with the Orejuelas of Cali and a few others, who ran the whole United States–bound market. Flowers were his favorite system. Colombia's a big producer, you see: biodiversity and all that crap. Flowers are a significant item on the national balance sheet. He used to fill the flower containers with powder and send them north by plane. If you controlled the customs offices, that was possible.

What's more, Don Pablo realized before anyone else that the promised land was Mexico. He felt restricted by his own system, even though it was huge and involved landing strips in the jungle, light aircraft, motorboats, and even a submarine that shuttled to California. He had even grander ideas. So when he finally succeeded in getting into Mexico, he planned things carefully.

It wasn't easy to establish yourself there. The local traffickers are fearsome people, very violent, drug addicts, pitiless murderers, guys who torture people for the fun of it. They're different from the Colombians and from the South Americans in general—more mystical, perhaps. They make an industry out of their saints great and small, and they really believe in it, and witchcraft is part of the pact of membership and the rites that make them feel invincible. Witchcraft, well-oiled guns, and control of the border: they gave Don Pablo a lot of trouble. But he had the strength of *la plata*—silver, cash—and he knew how to use it. He also knew that money is not enough. You need a symbol. You have to be able to flaunt the greatness of your power and your wealth if you're to earn your rivals' respect. So to conquer Mexico, he needed some spectacular success. He used to send the stuff to Tijuana by truck, in fairly small quantities. Crossing the land border with the United States has always been a rather trickier business than getting through airports. To transport the cocaine, Escobar's organization used compartments built into the big gas tanks of the tractor-trailers that ply the Pan-American Highway. When the vehicle got to the other side, someone dismantled the gas tanks and replaced them. A short-lived trick, it didn't take much to see through it. Then Don Pablo started sending merchandise in tankers too. But that wasn't a difficult system to break either. At customs they had only to check how many gallons had been declared, and with a few measurements and a simple calculation, they discovered the anomaly.

One day in Ciudad Juárez, Don Pablo Escobar had the idea of his life. To tell the truth, he had the idea of his life every week, and not all of them were that great. But this time he really did think up an amazing scheme. First of all, he erected a big building materials store at El Paso, on the Texan side of the border. Operating through the usual front men, of course. Like every self-respecting drug smuggler, he had plenty of dollars in ready cash: about fifteen billion dollars, as a matter of fact, equivalent to the GDP of a small nation.

The money was handled according to Don Pablo's usual methods. He kept it in big ventilated rooms, underground vaults equipped to prevent the damage that comes with prolonged storage. The banknotes were vacuum-packed but humidified so they wouldn't crumble. It was expensive, but not as expensive as having your money intercepted. Vacuum packing is a method we still use today. A parcel of money shrinks to an incredibly small size; you can practically get half a million dollars in your pocket. Because money's bulky stuff. You won't believe this, but when I used to travel around with suitcases full of payments, I was more scared than when I carried cocaine. Here too there are myths you've got to get out of your head: phantom finance companies, Chinese boxes, hidden transactions, cyberfinance. In our line of business, payment is strictly in cash, and it's certainly a problem. Don Pablo always used one-dollar or twenty-dollar bills because they arouse fewer suspicions. When you work with those denominations, however, the bulk is considerable, even in vacuum packs.

Anyway, after building the store in El Paso, Don Pablo starts buying up plots of land in Juárez, and there too he sets up a little building materials business. Then he spends a year and an enormous number of dollars digging a two-mile tunnel equipped with air-conditioning, silent transportation by means of rubber trolleys, and a system of halogen lighting. A technological jewel that cuts like a razor through the most closely watched border in the world. He scatters the earth that's dug out of the tunnel on the surrounding desert or carries it away in covered trucks. He uses teams of laborers, technicians, and engineers, different companies for each stretch of a few dozen yards, so that nobody really understands what the project is or what route the tunnel follows. That's an old trick used by military architects in times gone by when building underground fortifications in order to keep the secret of their countermine defenses.

Of course, if you work that way, you can't be absolutely sure you've pointed the tunnel in the right direction, but Don Pablo is a lucky man, and he hits his Texan store on the other side of the border dead center. Enormous amounts of cocaine pass under there. The tunnel is equipped with a system of pulleys for loading and unloading, which Don Pablo likes to call "the horizontal elevator." The whole thing is a technological marvel. It doesn't last, though. The entire investment falls foul of the usual banal, goddamned tip-off. The Americans have noticed that masses of stuff are arriving, the consumption and seizure figures have shot up, and the wholesale price per kilo on the Texan market falls in a very short time from 13,000 dollars to 6,500 dollars, half the amount. So the DEA, the American antidrug agency, and the FBI start looking for a deep throat.

Given the pharaonic methods of Escobar and of his times, it wasn't hard to find a little birdie willing to sing. "Take it easy," someone should have told him, but Pablo Escobar wasn't the kind of guy who takes it easy. In any case, he heard about the tip-off in time and had the whole thing dismantled, so in the end all they found was a hole, no trace of his science fiction installation. Even today very few people know what really went on down there. Even in the dismantling, Don Pablo's work was masterful. The project, however, was finished. It was time to think up something new: new in conception, not in the quantity and the methods.

At the time, most Colombian merchandise started its journey from Buenaventura. There was a fair degree of agreement among the cartels about sharing the logistical platforms, such as the port of departure, the port of arrival, and the docks. And these were lucky times; never had the United States represented a less serious problem. This was when cocaine was being procured from the Colombian cartels to finance the Contras in Nicaragua. They needed us. But Pablo Escobar wanted to become a parliamentary deputy. He had high ambitions, and among the other disasters that this lust for power brought upon him was a war with Cali, which led to slaughter on a massive scale.

During the conflicts between the two big cartels, someone even founded a national association for victims' relatives. Too much bloodshed, too much visibility, and, as if that wasn't enough, everything was ruined by the scandal of the so-called Iran-Contra affair, when the news broke of the triangular trade whereby the United States funded the Nicaraguan rebels through its supposed enemy in Asia.

The United States Versus Don Pablo

When the story of this trade between angels and devils got out, it opened the floodgates. The age of the War on Drugs began, and the DEA started setting up bases in Venezuela and Colombia and infiltrating men into the plantations, overflying vast swaths of the continent and spraying them with defoliants and some of the most poisonous chemical agents in existence. They had satellite guidance and easily found the landing strips, the fields, and above all the big kitchens (the workshops where the basic paste is refined). They made widespread use of herbicides, devastating fertile areas, ruining farmers in the tens of thousands, and driving them into the arms of my colleagues in order to survive.

Certainly, if a guy can earn in three months from a hundred grams of coca what he would earn in five years from tons of rice, it's obvious that replacing the coca crops with something different is an idea that could have been dreamed up only by a bunch of smart-asses used to taking the elevator down from their glass towers in New York to lunch on expensive raw fish in the sushi bars of Manhattan.

The yield of coca is different from that of soya, for example, even assuming that soya is suited to the same kinds of soil as coca. It's important to remember that our little plant is self-fertilizing—it clears the land where it grows of weeds and makes it fertile for a new sowing. It's perfect for mixed crops (which also happen to be very useful for hiding it: one row of coca and one of French beans, for example), and for renewing the harvests. To insist on its being replaced by other plants that may poison the land, as some fruit trees do (in Italy the walnut, for example), is to kill the farmers, wipe out the villages, desertify the valleys. It's a policy like the one the Soviets used to adopt when they needed to get rid of a few million nomads in Central Asia. Their method was to introduce a monoculture of cotton, say, so that the people would die of starvation. It never failed.

You might find it amusing that UN officials and American free traders work in the same way as the Soviet Communist Party. The difference between starvation and life doesn't even cross their minds. They're no better than we are, even if they cut an impressive figure with their tweed jackets, their big ties over their blue shirts, and their brows eternally furrowed from worrying about the welfare of the Third World poor. A lot of people have made a lot of money out of it. Under the pretext of eradicating coca from the Bolivian mountains, certain Italian and Swiss firms—including one well-known confectionery company—got their hands on huge areas of pasture for their animals, only to back out later because cattle don't thrive at those altitudes.

Anyway, Bush senior's War on Drugs forced the plantations to move into the woodland and spread out across the territory—in a word, to expand. And to come into contact with all the crooks who roam the forest, such as the guerrillas, who had to finance themselves, and certainly not with money of legal provenance. And the antiguerrillas too. Do you know who the worst bastards in the world are? The paramilitaries, the guard dogs of the big emerald traffickers. A narco can't stand those guys, but he'll do business with them. Cocaine became the means of exchange for all the business of the militaries, para-militaries, and *fazendeiros*—for paying private bodyguards, for everything, everything you could possibly imagine, whether beautiful or ugly, ideal, filthy, or normal. And things became more refined: the producers tried to concentrate the whole cycle of the merchandise, as happens in other industries. Every-one looked after his own little quota, trying to bring it as safely as possible to the market, finished, ready for consumption.

By that time nobody could make a living without coca. The only alternative was to emigrate to the United States. Maybe to Miami, a city built on cocaine, constructed with the money from laundering, kept alive by the banks that processed the narcos' money. A never-ending circle. But although it's easy for money to get into Miami, for an aspiring laborer or unskilled worker it's a different matter. He's driven to illegal immigration, and that can end very badly. They'll let your dollars in, but when you come along in person, they're not interested. During that period the people who did real business were the good guys. It's always been like that, really: 95 percent of the wealth created by the distribution of cocaine ends up in the banks of the rich countries; the producers are left with the crumbs and the blame. The World Bank and the International Monetary Fund had dozens of projects, all at government level. They fi-nanced friendly governments, for example, donating five hun-dred million dollars for development, which—the day after it was delivered to some suntanned and trusted president—had already returned home to some bank in Miami. Besides, who would seriously have invested in the development of countries that had no infrastructure? It was a farce. Useful for political relations, for military control, and for economic influence. Call-ing it the War on Drugs added a pinch of symbolic pepper, but the truth is, it was precisely that policy which made cocaine the sole basis of all trade, and certainly not to the benefit of the starving farmers.

And—can you believe this?—sometimes it was the narcos themselves who got angry about it. Pablo Escobar, for example, was an idealist in his way. And for this very reason he catastrophically overreached himself. He said he was willing to pay off his country's foreign debt. How about that for ambition! Thirty billion dollars. Utter bullshit, of course. But embarrassing for everyone. A populist move, but one that dramatically highlighted the huge gap between the statements of the great and good of the world and their actions. In fact, he and his partners really did possess at least half that sum between them. Money's not something to be taken lightly, even if you have more of it than a fifth of the states in this world.

Don Pablo had conceived the crazy idea of going into politics himself, of gaining power and administering it. A mistake that every good drug smuggler nowadays knows mustn't be made. Politics won't bother you if you don't bother it. It allows you to work, takes its own slice, and doesn't touch yours, but if you try to oust it, it remembers that it's a military force. The holder of a monopoly on violence. For Pablo they set up the *bloque de búsqueda*, a special search unit just for him, comprising the finest uniformed assassins on the continent. They fired two missiles at him, devastating eleven apartments. An Israeli-style operation, you might call it—one of those targeted murders with collateral damage that occurs every day somewhere on the planet. But this one irreversibly changed the world of the underground economy.

Today there's a stoic element in the makeup of every true drug smuggler. He lives in hiding; his aim is to be as inconspicuous as possible. The so-called empire of drugs is far more complex than the criminal organizations that form a part of it.

It's a global economic system that includes other elements that draw on it in abundance: the police forces, the world of politics, the national and international agencies, the NGOs that combat drug smuggling—and the banks. What would become of beautiful Miami, with its palms, everglades, restaurants, and promenade, if it weren't for our dollars? I'll tell you: there would be a collapse, a crash on the scale of the one that occurred in Argentina. That world wouldn't exist without us, and believe me, it will never really try to destroy us unless we threaten other people's roles within the system.

Everybody has his own place. The politicians do the politics, we deal with the money side, and the do-gooders provide the goodness. And so we'll go on forever. Escobar didn't understand that. Orejuela, Don Gilberto of Cali, had a more modern approach. He knew how to diversify his investments, and he always had a very relaxed relationship with the political world. Ochoa and Cardona were the same. All these guys gradually came to understand that the narco's highway runs parallel to the highway of politics, it doesn't cross it. With Ochoa and Cardona comes the birth of modern, integrated drug smuggling. And through family ties and marriages, the shadow of Cardona stretches over the only empire that still exists today, the Guajira. The grand old men all live happily in New York—not in hiding on some small reservation in the jungle—and direct operations from a taxi or a plane, hunted by the authorities yet invisible to them. To some extent, things have been complicated for them since September 11, with the antiterrorism legislation, the fingerprinting, and all that stuff. Previously in the United States you could catch a plane the way you caught a bus; now everything's a bit more difficult. Now they check your fingerprints, search your luggage, even look inside your underpants. And in the ports there are the scanners, the electric arches. They're a nasty problem, but if you stick it out to the end of my course, you'll learn how to deal with them.

The Cali Cartel at Work

With the fall of the cartels, the size of the shipments changed too. In Escobar's day it was quite normal for those who could afford it to organize shipments of four or five tons. It was the age of spectacular schemes: the tunnel, the submarines. Don Pablo was even able, through an agreement with the Cuban government, to control military bombers, which would take off from Isla de Pinos and dump the merchandise, packed into floats, off Miami. They were picked up by the cartel's men in fast, maneuverable Cigarette boats. They had a special technique: they would spread out in a ring around the prearranged dropping ground, then shoot off in different directions and slip into the maze of swamps in the Everglades, where they couldn't be pursued. It was quite a sight. Imagine an enormous star resting on the surface of the ocean. The packages fall in the center, they're picked up, the stuff scatters in all directions and disappears into the swamps. The risks were pretty low, on the whole. One guy even bought himself a small island in the Bahamas. It was eight nautical miles from the North American coast, and with the speedboats you could carry the stuff right to the homes of the Yankees along the Miami River. Later it became almost impossible to carry more than two hundred or three hundred kilos at a time. At least by sea. Until the invention of the darkness.

But when people began to realize that the traditional modes of transportation were running into trouble, they proceeded by trial and error. Poetic stuff, don't you think? The prose was us, later. Efficient prose too, to the tune of billions, but you still can't help feeling nostalgic for those romantic times. Pablo Escobar's main competitors were the Orejuelas of Cali, the most powerful cartel in the world (that's who I started out with, at the beginning of my career). The boss of the cartel, in the golden age, was Don Gilberto Orejuela, who was as imaginative as Pablo, a genius at improvisation and at organization. A maestro. A story that sums him up pretty well is the affair of the Panama crane.

There was a project undertaken about twenty years ago by a certain North American state—okay, Georgia—down on the Panama Canal. Infrastructure works, major building projects entrusted to private American firms with the endorsement of the Panamanian state. Their particular specialty was wide-span bridges. They needed huge telescopic cranes, hundred-ton monsters that weren't easy to come by in Central America. Indeed, the state of Georgia had to supply them to the general contractor, the private firm that organized the works and awarded subcontracts to smaller firms. Two huge telescopic cranes.

The work was soon completed, successfully and to the great satisfaction of the local and American firms and the authorities. The next job was to get the cranes back home to Georgia. It was given to an American freight company. No special security measures were taken. After all, who's going to steal them? Forty-eight hours before the cranes are due to leave, in the middle of the night, a few guys drop in on the night watchman, asking for the person in charge of the transportation of the cranes.

A team: decisive, professional, and calm. Some of them stay with the night watchman, who, naturally, doesn't take five seconds to provide the name and address requested, while others dash to a hotel in the capital to make the American contact in charge of the shipment an offer he can't refuse: either we kill you right now, or we put five hundred kilos of cocaine into the main arm of one of the cranes. "I don't particularly want to die," the Yankee must have said, or words to that effect, and then, since he wasn't a fool, he probably added, "At least tell me how much I get out of it." The reply was very tempting: Not only do you get a kickback, but you know what we'll do? We'll give one of the cranes a nice hard bash, damage it, and buy it back from you. That way you'll get something for the scrap value too. And that way the Cali boys—you'd guessed who it was, hadn't you?—will have access to the stuffed crane so that they can unload it and dismantle it themselves.

The next evening, as arranged, about twenty people turn up at the depot and get to work. They organize a collision between the two cranes, a carefully aimed blow. One of the cranes falls over with its arm extended, and it's impossible to close it again. A damage assessment is immediately carried out by Panamanian officials whose palms have been crossed with dollars, and meanwhile, inside the two central columns of the crane with the jammed arm, our Colombian friends find fabulous cavities—Ali Baba's cave. There's room for a special shipment in there: two and a half tons. It'll make the five hundred kilos they'd been planning look like chicken feed. To pack in the merchandise, they'll need two days, but departure will have to be postponed anyway. The problem is that the stuffed crane really is damaged, and there is no way of closing that damned telescopic arm. There's only one solution: little by little, as the tube is filled, bits of the arm are cut off. In the end the crane looks as good as new and sets off for Savannah together with its pristine twin.

The border crossing is easy. The crane is state property, so there are no special checks. The state authorities are reimbursed for the damage to the crane by the insurance company. But there's a hitch. The crane is not for sale. It's Georgian law: state property that has to be sold off must go to auction. Now, the Colombians aren't vindictive. They don't kill people for a simple mistake or to vent their frustration when a deal turns out to be unexpectedly complicated. Not immediately, anyway. In this case the cartel decides that it can't blame the Yankee who made the agreement; he couldn't have foreseen this quirk in the state laws, and after all, he's lost out too, because he won't get anything, apart from the original bribe. And his life, of course. So there's nothing for it but to take part in the auction. The trouble is, it's extremely difficult to cheat in an auction organized by an American state. The boys consider the matter. Should they find a front man and get him to buy the crane? That could be very expensive. So they decide to stand by and watch. They'll attend the auction to see who buys the iron colossus.

A wrecker. That's who wins—a wrecker from Oklahoma. The crane is motorized, it moves. It'll be a slow journey, but it's doable, thinks the cowboy, and he heads off westward with his crane. Slowly. He's feeling hungry, so as soon as he gets beyond the borders of Georgia, he stops for a meal in a Longhorn on the interstate highway. Barely ten minutes later some polite-looking, rather suntanned guys come in, sit down at his table, and strike up a conversation. It doesn't take them long to come to the point.

"We're in love with the crane. We're collectors. We want to buy it."

"Not on your life. I've waited years for a chance like this. I'm not selling."

"What? Not selling? You can only gain from it, you know.

We can give you a good bargain, not like those thieves in the Georgia state administration. We know the real reason it broke down: it was defective in the first place. They've sold you a pup, friend."

"Nothing doing. I know about these things, guys. That crane's a beauty, and I'm keeping it."

The boys think about it some more. The problem is not insoluble, but a murder in a Longhorn on an interstate highway causes a stir, attracts attention. That would be a problem. And then, after the deed, making off in that lumbering vehicle . . . No.

They let him go, and the cowboy travels back to Oklahoma at a very leisurely pace, with the Colombians still on his tail, looking forward to the great moment. Soon it will be time to see that magnificent steel arm in action. The cowboy turns the key; the arm's little motor sputters but doesn't fire. Of course it doesn't, because there's no pressure in the hydraulic system that powers the arm. There's cocaine inside it instead of oil.

Purely by chance, like in the cartoons, two experts in hydraulics pass by. The United States is a big country. Why shouldn't two experts in hydraulics with healthy complexions be out for a stroll at that time of day and outside that compound? "We'll repair it. But we'll have to inspect it in our workshop. Back home in Houston."

So the crane makes another interstate trip, destination this time, Houston, Texas. The problem for the boys now is: Do we really fix it and give it back to the cowboy, or do we shoot him in the head?

Difficult decision. To clarify their thinking, they drop in at the Komatsu dealer for the spare parts. The Komatsu technician looks at the crane and, as dollar signs light up behind his glasses, suggests replacing the cylinder. For a mere 450,000 dollars, a snip. The whole crane is worth 200,000. At that time co-caine on the U.S. market sold at about 13,000 dollars per kilo, wholesale. There were two and a half tons of the stuff inside there. Well okay, we'll have the repairs done and call the guy from Oklahoma to come and pick it up. He comes and can't believe his eyes: "Wow, what a beauty!" But at this point the Cali boys have got to pull out at least one painful tooth. You can't work like this—spend half a million dollars and just keep your mouth shut.

They're furious with the Japanese guy from Komatsu. You know how it is. The big fish wins, the little one loses out and wants to recoup his losses. The Colombian boys don't know where they stand in the food chain now, so someone has got to pay to reestablish order. What is this? We're giving hundreds of thousands of dollars to a guy who has spent no more than eighty thousand to get the crane. That's ridiculous! We told him it was a minor problem; we can't come along now as if nothing has happened and present him with the real bill. He'd realize something funny was going on. Who cares? We can make him, too, an offer he can't refuse, but a generous one, not a rip-off: a contract to lease the crane for five years, which includes paying the people who did the repairs.

The problem seems to have been solved, but they've forgot-ten all about the other crane, the undamaged one. The one that was supposed to remain virgin. The trouble is that one of the Cali guys, a small-time crook in his own right, had had the bright idea down in Panama of inserting a little operation of his own into the big operation, and we hid his cocaine in the tool-box of the control cabin. Not much: 150 kilos—150 kilos of co-caine! Unknown to the bosses. Take note: one of the most serious dangers when you send a shipment is that one of your men will slip his own junk in among your stuff. Or worse, that the person you're working for will think it's you who's trying to pull a fast one. It's essential that the quantity on arrival and the quantity on departure should be absolutely identical. It's a question of professional ethics. It's only with this kind of scrupulousness, obsessively adhered to, that you gain your client's confidence.

The trouble is that the crane belongs to the state and is in good working order, so it's liable to be called into service whenever there's a need. Well, a need arises at once, and the crane leaves before the small-time crook or anyone else has been able to unload it. The guy sees what's happening, gets scared, says nothing, and simply gives his 150 kilos of powder up for lost. A big mistake. Somebody opens the crane, finds that treasure trove, and calls the DEA. The first thing the DEA does, naturally, is to go and pick up the American contact who had been in charge of the work in Panama (the one our friends from Cali had called on in his hotel), give him a good going-over, and throw him into a federal prison in Florida, just in case he should feel like talking.

The second thing they do is to start looking for the other crane.

The DEA agents arrive in Oklahoma and hear the story of the broken arm, and it doesn't take them long to reconstruct the monster crane's route. They dash down to Texas, and in Texas they learn that the crane has been repaired. They see it. It's clean. They do nothing. Nothing. They just wait and watch. Never underestimate those DEA guys, they're not as stupid as you wish they were. And even when they're corrupt, there's always a chance one of them will be more interested in the kudos of a nice fat seizure or a prestigious arrest.

The news travels fast, and the feeling that he's got away with it goes to the head of the small-time crook who lost his

150 kilos and needs to recoup his own losses. So he has a very bad idea, an even worse idea than putting his stuff in with an Orejuela shipment. I'll call on Don Gilberto, he thinks, and blackmail him. A suicidal scheme, but one that has some prospect of succeeding owing to an excess of thoughtfulness on the part of Don Gilberto. This little punk can't be so stupid as to blackmail me, thinks the old boss. There must be something else behind it. He suspects that the DEA has got something on him. He has the whole itinerary of the cranes retraced, to see if he's left any clues, and decides that the only person who could know anything, apart from his most trusted associates, is the American contact in the prison near Miami. An unlucky man. Don Gilberto's killers go looking for him in the United States. Killing a guy in jail is even easier and cheaper than doing it on the outside. You can always find someone who's willing to do the job for you, and he probably won't ask for more than a couple of cartons of cigarettes. But Don Gilberto scents a trap; he's convinced the Yankee is collaborating. They're trying to lead me on, he thinks. This calls for a countermove, so the big boss turns to a well-known Miami lawyer who specializes in drug smuggling and asks him to make a few inquiries. It doesn't take much for an old fox to find out that the guy they're looking for is in a federal prison and that he doesn't have any protection. He's unprotected, therefore he's not a collaborator. The lawyer has him contacted in prison by some of his clients (he has clients everywhere), the guy swears he hasn't squealed, and "prison radio" confirms this. Then the lawyer manages to get hold of the papers on his case and sees that the Yankee is not lying. Don Gilberto is puzzled.

But either you do things *al brinco rabioso*, or as time passes, even the biggest imbecile understands that something is not going right. In our case the imbecile is the guy with the

150 kilos who tried to blackmail Don Gilberto. He notices that nobody is answering him and guesses that something's up. He immediately flees to Miami, hoping to blend in with the crowds up there. But he forgets about his parents in Colombia, and after all, even a patient guy like Don Gilberto has his limits. So the first time our friend hears from his parents is when they are tied to two chairs in front of a thug from Cali who's holding a big knife in one hand and a telephone in the other and has just told them, "What a pity to have to die, and die such a nasty death, when you're innocent. Let's give your son a call." They're reluctant, but the thug can be very persuasive: "We could always write him a lot of nice little letters and put a little piece of mama or papa in every envelope." Better the phone call. The message is: we're old, the problem isn't dying, it's how we die.

The son understands. He takes the first plane for Bogotá, making an appointment to meet the Cali people in the arrivals hall at the airport, but he also arranges to meet a friend of his, who joins him there and immediately slips him the gun. Then he stands in the middle of the hall and looks around. As soon as he's sure the Cali guys are watching, he pulls out the pistol from under his T-shirt and shoots himself in the mouth.

The moral? You want a moral from this story?

A Question of Credibility

A debt to a narco is undoubtedly a problem. And a serious problem at that. But it's not the way you see it in the cinema: you've lost us some money, so a killer arrives, makes you suffer a bit, and then kills you. That's the way of the Serbs, the Mexicans too. In South America, killing a debtor is either an act of folly or the last resort, the very last. The priority is not punishing; it's getting your money back. It's the sunny side of the narco. He doesn't have a code of ethics or a hierarchy of principles to enforce. What counts is money and all the pleasure you can get from it. Nothing else. So first comes the seizure of possessions, and then, if the guy has nothing worth seizing, slave labor: you're going to do for me everything I need you to do, from surveillance to collection to the occasional bit of intimidation in town, until I've recovered what you owe me. Then, if it's really unavoidable, well, here the problem changes, because now it's a problem of credibility, and credibility is crucial in business. In fact we do have a kind of ethical code of our own. If you fail, but you've worked well, have done everything right, and are not to blame, you don't pay. This enables you to work with a certain degree of freedom. There have been exceptions, it's true, but in the end they cancel themselves out. For example, there was a woman, known as "la Sanguinaria," who operated in the Darién Gap, on the Panamanian border. She was a natural leader but way too violent. She didn't allow any exceptions to her rules, and she never forgave. She was quite capable of shouting in an old professional's face things like "I don't give a damn about your excuses! You've got to pay!" She was vulgar. But one day she offended a friend of Pablo Escobar's, and they had her head chopped off. Just like that. No more, no less.

As for the crane guy, he did something quite outrageous: he shot himself in El Dorado International Airport in Bogotá. Which is teeming with DEA agents and informers. Let's spell it out in business terms: all the U.S. general contractors who work in South America will stop buying their machinery abroad, and in the event of importation—sometimes it can't be avoided—they'll impose strict controls on local operators. So, at the end of this long story, who made the billions? Caterpillar Brasil, Ltda.

That's the way of the world.

In short, the bosses of the big cartels were very inventive people, capable of finding unexpected solutions, skilled and flexible enough to sail their way across the sea of money and problems that cocaine produces, and yet these qualities weren't enough for survival. The fragility of the bribery-based system was in danger of sweeping away the whole white powder economy at the very time the doors of Europe were opening. Something else was needed, something more radical. The time of the *sistemistas* had come—people like me, who ply the trade I'm going to teach you. But in the late 1980s the big cartels, the ones that made the real money circulate, weren't used to turning to a specialist in delivery systems. Their approach was very simple: first, produce; second, sell at once. And the method best suited to this approach was the old one—greasing, oiling, bribing. But this approach was getting them into trouble.

Even giants fall, then, and they make quite a noise. It was after the fall of Pablo Escobar, roughly speaking, that the war among the cartels began. His death in 1993 created a vacuum that everyone competed to fill. Each cartel had its own agreements with the authorities, each cartel tried to pay its own officials, and one of the main objectives of each cartel was to give satisfaction to the DEA or the FBI. To avoid publicly embarrassing them and to save their own skins. Of course, the problem was solved at their competitors' expense. If you can put a rival's merchandise in the hands of the cops, you've hit the jackpot. They leave you alone, and someone else suffers.

Admittedly, in the heat of the competition some pretty

rough methods were used, as in the never wholly explained case (but now I'm going to tell you what really happened) of the archbishop of Guadalajara.

A Martyr to Drug Smuggling

Monsignor Posadas Ocampo, archbishop and cardinal, was killed on May 24, 1993, at Guadalajara International Airport by fourteen bullets that pierced his armor-plated car. Ocampo was included by John Paul II in the list of the martyrs of the twentieth century, and rightly so. He had distinguished himself in the fight against drug smuggling and has become a symbol. El Negro and El Güero, two bosses of the Juárez cartel, were accused of his murder, but things aren't as simple as the hagiography and the judicial verdicts make them seem. The fact is, the cardinal didn't know he was nurturing a serpent in his bosom.

At that time there was a war between the Payáns and the Rodríguezes, the two most influential families in the Mexican cartels. Both families worked in Baja California and in Tijuana. Like Don Pablo Escobar, they were tunnel enthusiasts. There was a Mexican, married to a Calabrian woman, who handled, on the Rodríguez family's behalf, the transportation of merchandise from Puerto La Cruz, in Venezuela, to Tijuana, the main route to the U.S. border. One day our friend is approached by certain *matones* employed by the Payáns, who make him their offer: we want you to take some shipments for us, together with your own shipments, on your usual route. *Matones*, guys who will kill you without a second thought, if doing so won't harm their boss. Our man is scared, but he has a problem. He works for the Rodríguez family, so he can't say no, but he can't say yes either, and what's worse, he can't explain why.

"I can't take them to Tijuana for you. I have to do some jobs up there for someone else. But if you want, I'll take them as far as Guadalajara."

He must have been very worried about replying like that to the *matón*, but evidently the *matón* had been prepared for it, because unexpectedly, he accepts. So our man starts transporting for the Rodríguezes to Tijuana and for the Payáns to Guadalajara. The shipments go smoothly until one day someone brings him a message from the Payáns: "We haven't got time to pick up the stuff at Guadalajara and take it to Tijuana this time. You must do it. You must at least get closer. Let's say this: you take it to the outskirts and then we'll take it into town."

Again, an offer that can't be refused. A very difficult situation, with five hundred kilos of pure cocaine at stake.

Before you enter Tijuana from the south, there's a tunnel. He arrives there with his men and with his trucks well filled. But the tunnel is barred by the Feds. This means big trouble. The Payáns, who are following, to keep a check on him, think it's an ambush that he has arranged with the Rodríguezes to block the shipment. A terrific *balacera* breaks out. People start shooting from all directions. Everyone at everyone else. In the end our man is captured, and off to jail with him go some of the Payáns' men, who, naturally, once they get inside, try to bump him off. He's shitting himself, and this time he does appeal to the Rodríguezes. They knew all about it, and he knew that they knew, so the conversation must have gone roughly like this: "I was only carrying cocaine for those guys, do you understand? Transportation and nothing else. And you allowed me to do it, so now it's down to you to save my ass from the Payáns."

The Rodríguezes think about it and decide that he's right. By wholesale bribery they manage to get him out. The jails all over Latin America are open systems; inside you're in contact with everybody. And inside, the narcos are not at war with other narcos. They're at war with robbers, common criminals. In Tijuana prison, however, one of these robbers is on the payroll of the Rodríguezes. At their request, he offers our man his protection. But the man is scared to death; he thinks it's a dangerous sign. As soon as I get out, they'll kill me, he thinks. Things are complicated by the fact that the five hundred kilos of stuff have disappeared. The Payáns haven't got them, the Feds haven't got them, our man hasn't got them. You have only to put two and two together. Who took the merchandise? The Rodríguezes, obviously. Their boss, El Gigio, is sitting on a mountain of dollars. With one part he pays his people, with the other he invests in more drugs or in real estate (the narcos' favorite kind of legitimate business). El Gigio's problem is that he has to invest the money in the United States if he wants it to earn really high interest. And who's going to take it over to the other side? A mountain of money that has popped up out of nowhere, the product of half a ton of snow that fell from the sky one fine summer's day. El Gigio, however, is a guy who knows how to organize, a forward planner, and he has a man in the curia too. In the curia, yes. No, I won't tell you who. All you need to know is that a gentleman in the pay of the Rodríguezes had a good position in the archbishop's palace. They called him Mr. Ten Percent, and we will too. Well, Mr. Ten Percent knows that Monsignor Posadas Ocampo is about to leave on a visit to the other side of the border. His armor-plated car will take him to the airport and then will be put, along with the prelate, on a freighter bound for the United States. Armor-plated because Monsignor Ocampo is a hero of the fight against drugs; therefore he needs protection. But what El Gigio thinks is: armor-plated, full of juicy little cavities, easy to fill. And safe: nobody will ever look in there, inside the monsignor's tank.

Now observe the scene carefully. The archbishop is on his way to the airport in his archiepiscopal Cadillac to begin a long pastoral visit to the United States. He doesn't know that everybody is at the airport and they're all waiting for his car. In the first place, the Payáns, who of course possess the means to ensure that they receive the right tip-off at the right moment and who therefore know what El Gigio Rodríguez is up to. A family of a hundred people, all determined to get their money back at any cost. And the Rodríguezes, present in force to protect the shipment. Naturally, as soon as the cardinal's armor-plated car appears, another fearful *balacera* breaks out. Again everyone shooting everyone else, and again many are left lying on the ground. Among them is the archbishop, martyr and future saint, because the rumor will soon spread that the gunfight was an attack on him.

When you kill an archbishop, it's hard to hush everything up, and when this point is reached, all the plans, the protection schemes, and the infiltrations are abandoned. The FBI realizes that the balloon is about to go up and cuts all its contacts inside the organizations. Balanced strategy doesn't matter now; the aim is to get them all, at once and in the same way, without diplomacy and without any consideration for one or the other. There are roundups, and as usual, large numbers end up in jail, but only very small fry. The person who pays for the broken dishes is the gunman. The bosses, as always, come out of it more or less spotless.

A moral again? There is no moral to be found in our stories. Only one fact: all it takes is a drunken customs officer boasting to a whore. Or a competitor's envy. Or an idiot who tries to make money by overcharging for the transportation. And even an empire capable of mobilizing ships and submarines, airplanes, big cranes, and mechanical diggers, building roads in the jungle and paying tens of thousands of men, collapses like a house of cards. There are mistakes that simply must not be made. Don Pablo's was to challenge the status quo in politics. He wanted to govern; he dreamed of becoming president and controlling the state, the police, the law courts, and everything else. But that's not the way for a long life. The secret is to stay on your side of the fence. To accept that you're a criminal. Anyone who crosses that line dies. Remember: you are not the law. The law is your antagonist, the other. And you must let the other play its own role. It's a balance that makes everyone rich. You never know, maybe the day will arrive when they need a few billion to flush out some modern-day Abu Nidal and they'll come and ask you for it.

LESSON TWO: Methods of Small-Scale Transportation

The Age of the Couriers

The fall of Cali and Medellín marks the beginning of the do-it-yourself age. Controlling the market becomes impossible, suddenly everyone has his own little company, dozens of mini-cartels spring up, and the structure of the organization changes. For example, the kitchens, which had previously belonged to the cartels, start to sell their produce independently to anyone who travels along the right routes. It's the beginning of the age of the suitcase-carrying courier. Bolivia and Peru, which had long been producers but had been marginalized by the Colombians, who controlled every outlet, step forward to take a major role, and our little plant starts being grown in Ecuador and in northern Argentina too. A new world opens up, a world that the United States would like to, and should, control.

Countless micro-organizations are formed, and for each

one, the whole production cycle is concentrated in one place, as far as possible. The refinement is done close to the plantation where the coca is grown. The kitchens scattered about in the jungle multiply, and the role of the international organizations, which had controlled the refining processes until the 1980s, decreases. For example, the Caruana-Cuntreras of Cosa Nostra, who originally handled the chemical processing of the product as well as selling it on the international market, from this time on become pure financiers. From every corner of the woods small quantities of merchandise spring up that need to be taken to the point of sale as safely as possible. It's the season of semi-artisanal methods, those that are still fashionable today among small producers and dominate the popular image of cocaine smuggling. The king of the low-profile methods is the courier, who is almost always very poor and often very creative.

Many think the stuff reaches Europe in the false bottoms of suitcases, in ovules swallowed by couriers, and in false teeth. That is not the case, and the main function today of the small couriers, the mules, is to be sacrificed on the altar of good relations with Western police forces. But the world of small-scale transportation is a training ground for everyone, an excellent experimental laboratory for methods of protection and modes of transport. It's the age of water (cocaine can be very effectively concealed in a liquid, which is evaporated when it reaches its destination, and it doesn't result in the loss of many of its alkaloid qualities), lead, graphite, and carbon paper. Of course, with these little systems you can't carry more than about fifty kilos at a time. You'll appreciate that a couple of two-ton deliveries a year makes more financial sense. A large amount guarantees fewer shipments, and therefore fewer risks, less visibility, and ultimately fewer problems. You're not on the market continually. Only once every five or six months. True, if you get caught on that one occasion, you make a very big bang, much louder than the three-year bang you make if they find ovules in your intestine.

How is an ovule made? It's not difficult: you roll some coca paste into a little ball, cover it with tinfoil, then cover the tinfoil with condom plastic, a tough material that is not easily corroded by acids and gastric juices. Then you cover the whole thing with beeswax, a substance the stomach won't reject. Well, that's one of the recipes, but everyone has his own specialist advisers and his own little secrets. Some good, some not so good. And when they're not very good, you can pay for it with your life. It happened to my friend Oscar.

Oscar used to supply the cocaine to a carabiniere, a very senior figure. One day Oscar says to me, "I need fifty kilos next Sunday."

I call my contact in the forest and ask him, "Shall we give it to him?"

"*Bueno.* At what price?"

"Well, he's a friend . . . And the other guy's a carabiniere . . . Not at market price, I'd say . . ."

"All right. But no less than fifteen thousand."

"Okay."

By doing them a favor, you get your hooks into them, you see? So if there's a carabiniere at some point in the chain, you give him a discount. Besides, I was fond of Oscar. At one point I even got him into the business of systems.

And Oscar liked me too. When I was finally arrested, he was determined to save my ass. He got me a couple of expensive lawyers, the kind who usually defend prime ministers or famous fashion designers in trouble. One guy in particular. No, I can't tell you his name, but think of someone famous, someone renowned for doing favors for clients—people who live abroad, for example. Anyway, I pay 130,000 dollars in cash into this mega-lawyer's Swiss bank account, and in exchange he saves a big slice of my ass, because at the trial he succeeds in getting them to drop the charge of criminal association for the purpose of drug smuggling. Involvement with the Mafia, that is, a charge that would have sent me straight to a special prison and the tomblike confinement known as "41-bis." And it's lucky I have an Italian passport, or no one could have got me out of there. It took a lawyer with balls of steel, because the prosecution had linked me to the Calabrians of Milan, the Serbs, and Michel Lanza's robbers in Marseille. Get locked up for that kind of thing, and they throw away the key. But the mega-lawyer succeeded in getting my case moved away from the Court of Milan, on the grounds that the container they intercepted had entered the country at Como. What a wonderful thing justice is! From that time on, I accepted all my responsibilities. In other words, I confessed everything; that way at least you get the case over with quickly.

Anyway, after I'd been sent to prison, a certain Marco, an important guy, calls my brother and says to him, "I owe your brother some money." This confession gives me great pleasure, not least because, to the best of my knowledge, this Marco is just about the only person in the world who doesn't owe me anything. After eleven years, the first time I'm allowed out on day release, he comes around to my house.

"How are you, my old friend?"

"Flat broke. Give me the money you owe me."

"That's why I'm here."

"Come on, I was only joking. You'd have to pawn your Land Rover . . . Tell me about Oscar."

"He's dead."

It was the first news to reach me since I'd emerged from the tomb of the living dead.

"What happened?"

Here's what had happened. Shortly after finding me a lawyer, Oscar got into financial difficulties and had trouble meeting the needs of his friend the carabiniere, so he flew to Colombia and went straight to see my contact in the forest. A very helpful person, kind—generous, even. But certainly not stupid. Still, he leaves a little door open for Oscar: "I'm not giving you any big coca, but for the sake of our mutual friend, every time you come here, I'll make you up some little balls if you want. You swallow them and you go home."

It's a good offer for someone who doesn't have many alternatives. You can take four hundred or five hundred grams every trip, at the very least. And Oscar wasn't the kind of guy who could get a bank loan to buy tons of cocaine. So I won't deny that the news came as a relief to me when I heard about it in jail. But although my contact was being generous, he gave Oscar only just enough coca to break even. I suggested to Oscar, who was too clever to spoil the plan, that he should carry cash instead: clean, easy, safe. But he thought that wouldn't be any fun. His stroke of luck, or his misfortune, was that he had a relative who worked as a steward on the Avianca service to Zurich. He thought he couldn't go wrong. But the trouble was, by this time he had a serious cocaine habit and had got heavily into debt. So one day, not so very long ago, Oscar makes another flight to Colombia. This was the part of the story I hadn't heard. He fills his stomach with ovules, but, like the fool he's always been, when he gets back to Italy, instead of shitting them out immediately, he simply changes planes and flies straight off to Warsaw, where he's got a girlfriend. Too much haste, too much greed: he can't even think about mundane things anymore, those things that anyone whose brain isn't gutted by cocaine knows perfectly well. Such as the way airports work. What with one delay and another, while he's waiting for a transfer somewhere or other, his bowels have done their work—even condoms can't hold out forever—and an ovule has burst inside him. He had twenty in his stomach. It's a horrible death.

It's the end of the mule.

What sort of person is he, the man who dies this death, the man with ovules in his belly? What kind of human being becomes a courier?

The Mules: Ovules, False Legs, and Buttons

The greatest of all the mules was "El Gordo" Rodríguez: an animal capable of carrying twelve hundred grams in his stomach and still having room to eat lunch during the flight. Stuffing yourself to the point of bursting with the precooked food they give you on the plane is a good way of allaying suspicions and reducing the risk of a check on arrival. But really, a kilo or two of cocaine, plus chicken curry, Tiger cheese, stewed pear, red wine, and lasagna al forno . . . If there's one reason for using the term "mule" for the couriers who use the ovule method, nobody has embodied it better than El Gordo. True, he got caught now and then, but he was a matchless artiste and knew how to turn the circumstances to his advantage. The main circumstance in his case being flab.

In the police offices in international airports there's a little toilet cubicle that has a net across the lavatory pan and a special little rake that is used by the officers who I imagine are the youngest ones: it is narco shit, after all. Then there are the X-ray machines (there I can see the old officers being deployed): they show how many ovules you have in your stomach. The old cop counts on the screen, then calls the young one and says to him something like this: "You've got to rake out at least fifteen . . ." But if you're fat enough, there's a chance something will get past the machine. Once, in Rome, El Gordo managed to keep a couple of ovules back and sell them in Regina Coeli prison, so he spent his regulation three years living like a king. Three years in jail is the norm if they find your ovules.

The mules' life is a pretty hard one. And, surprise surprise, the people who treat them worst are the Italians. Usually the promise sounds like this: "You carry a kilo to Europe for me and you get four thousand dollars: two thousand in advance and I'll deliver two thousand to your family." It's a kind of insurance. If the mule doesn't come back, he knows that at least his wife and children (there are always lots of children) have something to live on. Except that what really happens with the Italian narco is that first he cheats you on the two thousand greenbacks in advance. He buys you your ticket for the intercontinental flight and leaves you nothing but the change, if there is any. Peanuts. And then he doesn't give your family a penny. He has no intention of doing so; after all, who's going to check up on him? If the mule comes back and is still useful to him, then some money will reach his *mujer*, but if he gets caught—and he will get caught—he'll be reduced to poverty and his family will be ruined. Some contract.

That's what happened to El Gordo, even though he had in his pocket a nice little contract for 2,000 dollars up front and 2,500 dollars in favor of his Guajiro wife signed by an Italian narco based in Maracaibo. He was caught in Rome and didn't come back. He was ruined (except for the two little eggs he had managed to keep up his backside). And his wife let him know that she was finished with him and that she would never let him see his children again either. Even when he came back, there would be nothing for him at home. He was thirty-five and had been sentenced to three years in prison, but in a sense what he'd been given was a life sentence. El Gordo was the last person you would have suspected. He had eaten like a pig on the airplane and drunk whiskey throughout the trip, constantly pestering the hostess for more. And since he was a likable guy, he got double and triple rations. And yet before he had even walked down the steps from the plane, they were already waiting for him with a truncheon and an enema.

How come?

The mule is almost always a cover. The professionals, people with a suitcase or more, pass behind the mule. A *sistemista*, at any rate, never uses the methods of the small-time couriers, especially not the ovules. But bear in mind, if you're going to become a good *sistemista*, you'll have to be able to improvise, to respond to any request the client might make without any warning. You may have to get something through in a hurry, a modest quantity for urgent delivery. As a rule, it can take the *sistemista* as long as three or four months to organize a shipment, but sometimes he has to act quickly so as not to jeopardize the trust of a patron. Usually these sudden alarms involve only modest quantities, different from the ones the *sistemista* usually handles, but that doesn't mean he can afford not to respond to them. And in such cases there's nothing better than the pairing of mule plus serious courier: one with the little eggs in his stomach and the other with the suitcases. The function of the mule is to get caught.

So the best of them know this and make a profession of it. Like El Mocho: they called him that because he had only one leg. They used to make him another out of artificial flesh, beautiful, well lined, protected, perfect. He would put the cocaine inside it and set off happily for Europe.

And always get caught.

He did enough jail for a lifetime, in three-year spells. Spain, Portugal, Italy, Switzerland, all over the place. When he was in the Swiss prison, he didn't want to go home. He had grown contented and fat. He'd never felt like that in the barrio.

El Mocho was no fool. On the contrary, he was creative and a skilled tailor, so he invented a special method. He had a little machine for making buttons. He used to add thickener to the coca paste to harden it; then he would make buttons out of it. For his first trial run with this method he chose an easy flight: just over to Aruba. No dogs, no monitors, nothing. It was simply a question of whether or not the buttons would melt in the heat of the Caribbean. The trial run went without a hitch. But El Mocho was left with two problems, one unsolved, one unsolvable. The unsolvable one concerned the number of buttons: even if he took a large shipment of clothes, the most he could get into the buttons was one kilo six, one kilo seven. But he was given three-kilo commissions, and the only solution for those was the leg. So every now and then he would set off with his magnificent Bakelite limb bound for some European prison where he could spend three years without having to worry about his upkeep. El Mocho had no illusions about the contracts, and since he didn't have a family, he was content with the hope of being sent to jails like the Swiss one. The other problem remained unsolved simply because El Mocho couldn't be bothered to think about it: buttons are small and impossible to shield effectively, especially if they're passed through the sensitive scanners that are used to identify the merchandise. It wouldn't have been difficult to find a solution, though, if you gave it some thought. Just make a graphite bath and dip the buttons in it. Graphite makes an excellent shield. It looks black under the cocaine-spotting scanners in the airports, but black is a natural color for a button. When you have to protect a cake of coca paste, for example, a layer of carbon paper is always useful because it opacifies, like graphite. You wrap nylon around the cake, smear engine grease over the nylon, wrap carbon paper around the grease, and add more nylon, and your cake is pretty well covered. So all you'd have needed to do was dissolve the graphite and dip the buttons in it, and they would all have come out black, opaque to the sensors and also odorless, and therefore undetectable by dogs.

Do you know what always gives a mule away? His shoes. Brightly polished. Even El Gordo Rodríguez made that mistake. Usually he looked like the typical South American: slicked-back hair, expensive clothes . . . When he worked, he was pretty good at disguising himself, but he just couldn't do without his gleaming shoes. These are people who went barefoot for thousands of years. The discovery of the shoe was a milestone for them. You'll often meet a Señor Martínez or González in immaculately polished Italian shoes—Aldrovandi, Rossetti—walking through the forest. Those guys found me quite beyond the pale because I always wore tennis shoes.

So, find a down-and-out wearing shiny shoes and you have your mule, a cover figure at zero cost. You fill him up and then tell the relevant customs office that he's going to pass their way. They make a spectacular seizure, get in the newspapers, and someone's promoted, while you walk quietly past all the commotion carrying a shipment of a very different size. The police are quite happy to catch small fry. There's always a newspaper ready to lead with "Fifty kilos of cocaine seized. Worth . . ." Put any sum you like in the headline; after all, its only purpose is to create a sensation. The papers don't waste their time on reality. Astronomical figures for modest shipments, and the official gets some good publicity. Everyone's happy, and the market's inexhaustible, especially in the chaotic age of do-it-yourself and free-for-all. You'll always find something for yourself in all that confusion.

Besides, the mules are used to it. When they're caught, they always put on a great scene, acting like a character in some tragedy. In front of the policeman they generally tear their shirts. Watching them is like going to the theater: the cleverest ones cry real tears, and they all scream, *"Mátame! Mátame!"* Later, they put on another show at the trial. They all tell the same story: "I didn't want to carry the drugs, Judge, even though my family is starving! It was Commander X." Here you can add any name you want: any commander will do, guerrilla, paramilitary, or police. "He threatened us with guns: 'If you don't do it, I'll kill you all!' What could I do?" There you have it—always the same—the favorite excuse of all the mules in the world.

Pensioners and Phony Mothers-to-be

Now, how do you recruit a mule? Nothing could be easier on the streets of the barrio. I treat you to dinner, buy you a suit, another dinner, a few dollars in cash, and you're ready. There was a guy called Don José, a highly respectable middle-aged gentleman of Bogotá, who had his own specialty: elderly couples. He was successful for a long time with those little old ladies and gentlemen. He chose such dear old things, with such perfect faces you can't imagine. He would prepare the suitcases for them—three kilos per suitcase—and send them off to Zurich for a lakeside holiday. He loved retired professors and primary school mistresses: sweet faces, very well educated, and starving. He would give them two thousand dollars per kilo. So the old people would make twelve thousand dollars each, plus the trip, plus one night in a luxury hotel. They would travel from different places: once from Panama, once from Venezuela, another time from the Dutch Antilles. Many narcos used the system of package holidays. They would supply the tourists with specially prepared Samsonites: false bottom and false top. Very thin cavities. Then carbon paper and, on top, engine grease. Nobody takes hand luggage on package tours. The dogs don't smell anything, and the tourists have a free holiday. It was a good system.

Another good system, for a while, made use of women pretending to be pregnant, complete with artificial skin and three kilos of powder crammed inside. A smuggler from Monte Carlo used to sew it into the shoulders of his jacket: ten grams in each shoulder for a stay in Italy were enough for him. At one stage we used guys with long hair, putting rolled-up doses inside their dreadlocks.

I don't deny that even small-scale smuggling takes imagination, but these are all little systems suited to people who do it for pleasure, for themselves, the kind of people who put thirty grams in the handles of their briefcases. Even the nastiest cop isn't going to make a fuss about thirty grams. There are women who can get a hundred grams into their Tampaxes. At a retail price of fifty dollars per gram, one Venezuelan woman with a big pussy ended up carrying five thousand dollars in her knickers. A flight from Maracaibo to Miami costs three hundred dollars: you can work out the margin for yourself. A friend of mine once organized a shipment of *muñecas*, those terra-cotta Guajiro dolls. He took them to a duty-free shop in Zurich airport.

That was a pretty obvious ruse, though, and it would never have worked unless he'd bribed a few customs officers too.

There was also a guy who used to carry fourteen kilos in a pannier, during the summer, across the Andean passes between Chile and Argentina, a phony climber who lived in Mendoza. Nobody took any notice of him. At home he acted the starving climber; on the other side of the cordillera he was a millionaire. He got the pearly coca from a grower he could trust and made as much as a hundred thousand dollars a kilo. Climbing made him rich. He wasn't afraid of hard work, though. It would take him seven or eight days per trip, and he would travel to the pass by coach and then follow a sheep track through the woods.

But ultimately the little systems all have the same draw-back: sooner or later they get found out. In particular, imitation creates serious problems. The package-holiday method stopped working because it spread. Too many people were using it, in-cluding slapdash, unprofessional types. People who let them-selves get caught and would end up getting you caught too, if you weren't flexible. Genius consists in changing, in never standing still, in continually inventing new methods. The secret is always to stay one step ahead. And although the large-scale operations—the ones you'll hear about later—are the only true test of genius, there are still plenty of talented people even in the world of the small-time courier. My favorite was Renatino.

Renatino, a Courier with Style

Renatino the gentleman, ruined by dreams that at one point ac-tually came true, in the form of a luxurious German jail with all the creature comforts, and by a judge's promises. Renatino was another Italian, a guy who carried coca from Colombia to France using normal suitcases, a simple, effective method. He was always smartly dressed, impeccable, invisible. He had started out on his own in quieter times, but when the trouble started for him, he had been working so long that they were after him in France, always looking out for him. There were people determined to put him away for twenty years, but he always got through, every inch the perfect businessman, with that Italian flair for matching the hyacinth blue of his shirt with the dull blue of his suit, and coordinating ties. He used to carry four kilos in each suitcase—a small, unobtrusive amount—by Air France from Bogotá to Paris-Orly (De Gaulle got on his nerves).

Okay, the standard-size packet of coca, such as he used to carry, measures 15 centimeters by 7 centimeters by 6 centimeters. Do you see what I'm getting at? They're one-kilo cakes. You smear the cake liberally with engine grease, creating a uniform layer of 3 or 4 millimeters; then you cover it with plastic and cardboard, and on the outside you put an attractive gift wrap of the type sold in international airports, and maybe tie it up with a bow. That's basic protection for a courier.

With the money from his business, Renatino opened a restaurant in the Camargue in the South of France, at Saintes-Maries-de-la-Mer, a luxurious and tasteful establishment, and he married a Frenchwoman, a real beauty. They lived in the marshes—a lovely spot, apart from the mosquitoes—among mountains of salt and memories of the great massacre of the Piedmontese in the mid-nineteenth century, when the locals got tired of all those immigrants who worked in the salt flats—taciturn, jealous types, quick with the knife and a danger to the womenfolk. One night they decided to kill them all, even the women and children, and pursued them up the mounds of salt, slaughtering them with knives one by one. But that was a different world. Now Renatino was very comfortable there; nobody threatened him. He had a cozy, peaceful refuge, the right place for a guy who loves money and sailing. But he loved sailing too much. This is what happens: one day he buys a couple of boats and finds himself short. So what does Renatino do? He goes back to Colombia and starts playing the old game again. This time he finds a client, a real big one. A Romanian. You know how it is: narcos understand each other, they smell each other out at once. You like flashy things, eh? You're one of us, then . . . That kind of thing. This guy arrives with a diamond-studded Vacheron Constantin on his wrist worth seventy million lire and says he runs a crêperie. Ah, a crêperie! Let's talk business! So you casually say: "I spend my holidays in Colombia. I love the country, the seaside, the forest . . ."

And here you've dropped a nice little hint: Colombia.

"Heh, heh! Colombia! So you like sniffing!"

"Who, me? Have *you* ever tried it?"

The game begins, and goes on until he says, "Come round and see me sometime."

You go. Another casual, almost innocent chat.

"What part of the country do you go to?" he asks you.

"Villavicencio . . . La Felicidad . . ."

"Ah! Have you ever brought a little something back?"

"Presents, you mean?"

"Come on, be honest. How does it sell in Romania?"

"Fantastically well. If it costs twenty-five thousand dollars here, you can sell it for thirty-five thousand in Romania. Wholesale, no risks. What's more, the police don't know about it yet."

"You don't say! And . . . look . . . Who's going to go first, you or me?"

So Renatino volunteers. "I've got my own supplier at San José de Cúcuta. Good stuff."

It's agreed, the deal is done. For the first time in Renatino's career, it's with a client who's really worth serving. A real step up. The trouble is, the routes from Colombia are pretty closely watched, so the best course is to take the merchandise to Venezuela. It's not difficult. Cúcuta is quite near the border, level with San Cristóbal, but on the other side. You cross the border at San Antonio del Táchira. It's all forest and mountains there; a taxi never gets stopped, never. It's easy to organize. The transportation costs twelve hundred dollars a kilo. It's not difficult to get ten kilos across every two months. Then with the sale in Romania you make 350,000 dollars, and the 12,000 dollars you have to pay the people who carry the stuff across the border is small change.

In this job the expenses are always small change.

Provided the operation is successful.

Renatino and the Romanian form a partnership: 50 percent each. They buy themselves a beautiful flat in Bucharest, fill it with beautiful girls, real sluts of course, and start to live it up. Until one day, inevitably, along comes the *trampa*, the hitch, in the form of a suitcase that gets lost during a flight. Obviously at this point, when they find it for you, you're not going to go and collect it as any ordinary passenger would. You have to get rid of everything: flat, sluts, passports, identities, unsold merchandise, everything. A good drug smuggler always has five or six passports on him, so one down the pan is no problem. Even two or three unusable documents are no problem because you bought the flat with one passport, made the journey on another, and so on. But it's advisable to keep out of Bucharest for a while. So Renatino goes back to France.

Except that now he's made a name for himself, he has regular shipments and a pretty good clientele, and in those circumstances you often find someone who wants to raise the stakes. It's not long before he receives an order for a hundred kilos. A hundred kilos is on a different level, a level where it's no longer possible to play with chance—a professional affair, which needs careful preparation. There's one advantage, though: the supplier guarantees him transportation into Venezuela, to San Cristóbal, all expenses paid.

Renatino trusts him, a little too much perhaps, and goes down there with two Italian partners, experienced guys, to wait for the shipment. He takes a room in a nice hotel, one of those with a patio and a long wooden balcony looking onto a little square, with a flower bed in the middle so thick with vegetation it looks like ten square yards of rain forest, and you wouldn't be surprised to see a sloth hanging fast asleep from the eucalyptus trees. In those small mountain communities there are squares like that and hotels like that everywhere, and white churches and colonial-style town halls bathed in the sun, especially in the Cordillera de Mérida, south of the Maracaibo basin. Renatino loves it, revels in it. And revels in the local version of Cuba libre.

Then the Colombians arrive. Four or five, in a pickup laden with pineapples and bananas and fitted with drop-down sides. That's where the more valuable cargo is stored. It's a common trick. You get a good blacksmith to make you an underbar for the side about ten centimeters thick, and hollow. Inside it you put the cakes of coca, all tied together in a string, like those little salamis they make on the Po plain, so that you have only to tug and they all come straight out. The Colombians unload, as they always do, quite openly, as if everything were perfectly normal, in ten minutes flat.

And in ten *seconds* flat the police arrive and start laying into them as if they were beating sacks of hay. All of them, but especially the Colombians. The cops know that Renatino and his two friends are among them and give them their share: less than the Colombians, but there are still plenty of blows with the rifle butt for them too, on their bones and backs, like rain. They throw them into the cage-style police vans and leave them there without driving off—in the square, under the sun, waiting for the magistrate to arrive. The magistrate is needed so that they can be sent to Sabaneta prison, because Renatino and his partners are broke. Otherwise, with a bit of palm greasing here and a bit of sweet-talking there, something could have been worked out with those fine policemen, who, despite the tip-off they'd received, might still have been amenable to a discreetly offered bribe. But on this occasion Renatino and his mates have already blown all their money on Cuba libres and other distractions while they were waiting for the shipment. So as soon as the magistrate shows up, the police cars race off toward Sabaneta, to the joy of the newspapers, which put up big headlines about the "Italian drug-smuggling Mafia" on kiosks and crossroads all over Venezuela, as if to say, "We're honest people, but there's always someone coming in from outside bringing corruption."

Sabaneta. Nice jail. It's divided into three sections. The first houses the well-known narcos—the important, respected ones, almost all of them awaiting trial (after the trial they usually disappear). This is the best area of the prison, it's in good condition, it has everything: bathrooms, tiles, everything. Then there's the section where the scum live, which is again divided into two areas. On one side are the followers of the local boss—who in Renatino's time was a guy by the name of La Torre—and on the other those of the boss who wants to oust La Torre (or whoever his present-day equivalent may be). You soon realize that it's not in your interests to stay in the middle, and anyway they won't let you. It's either this side or that. And every evening they shoot at each other. There are no police or doors or bolts. Ah, the South American prison: a space isolated from society but, inside, completely open. People live together, invent rules for themselves. If you have money, you can get anything—weapons, good food, even women—and in the evening there's always a bit of a party based on lead and loud bangs, just to remind everyone where we are and whom we are with. So what do you do? You look for a place to sleep in some sheltered corner. But it would be a pity not to join the party. From nine o'clock in the evening anyone can enter the prison—women, and even children. People eat, dance, and make love. And shoot. Sometimes they shoot at the guards in the watchtower, who of course are only too happy to return fire and then, in the morning, calmly carry out the corpses in wheelbarrows. There's everything you could wish for inside.

Except water. Renatino takes the water from the toilets and allows it to settle, but that offers no guarantee of avoiding infection. Indeed, he falls ill, he can't stop crapping, he craps his guts out, pisses blood, spends every penny he has on antibiotics. He gets angry too. He protests, sends messages to the Italian embassy, which of course hasn't got off its ass (hardly surprising, with all those headlines about narcos and the Italian Mafia), but in the meantime he learns how things work. After all, far away from there he's a wealthy man. He arranges things and starts receiving a salary from home, one million lire a month. "Not much," you say. But it's enough to make him, in the space of six months, the richest man in Sabaneta. And in the meantime he's had a stroke of luck. The supervising magistrate is a woman of Italian origin. She seems to feel a kind of solidarity with him, and she arranges for him to be treated for his illness along with the other two Italians who have come down with the same ailments as Renatino. At the trial, though, he gets twenty years.

But he holds out. Having money sent in isn't difficult. You actually keep it in your pocket in prison. Not all of it, of course. Most of the money you entrust to a friend outside who occasionally hands some over, so that you never have so much that you risk arousing someone's greed and never so little that you can't pay for something. There's even a restaurant inside.

Italy doesn't lift a finger for guys like Renatino, it's true, but the funny thing is that the person who does come along is the French consul. He doesn't bring good news: "We know all about the Camargue and Romania. As soon as you come back, you'll get another twenty years in France." "Very kind of you to tell me, thank you; don't show your face around here again." The consul is an intelligent person, and having done his duty, he does indeed disappear for good. The important thing is that Renatino is forewarned. His problem now is surviving in a Venezuelan jail. There'll be time to think about Europe later. He's bright; he picks up Spanish very quickly and uses it effectively to ingratiate himself with both sides: the La Torre supporters and those of the other guy, who happens to be called Lluviano.

His first move is to buy two television sets and give one to each party. It works, and before long everybody likes him. He's performed the miracle of remaining neutral, a magic trick that, if you can pull it off, means no one can touch you. But it's still twenty years. He's forty. He has to get busy. So Renatino makes friends with the judge. He has a proposal for her: "The library needs reorganizing. I'll do it; I can turn my hand to anything." He gets a considerable degree of freedom. He goes to and fro from the prison, fits himself out a luxury cell with sanitary fix-tures, a washing machine, and a number of lackeys who scurry about in his service—his and that of the dollars he distributes. You can buy a man with fifty dollars in that place. He's got to the stage where he could move to the sector of the well-known narcos: luxury, quiet, and useful friendships. But he chooses not to. Because one day during one of these village festivals that take place at Sabaneta, half outside and half inside the prison, he's met the sister of an inmate who works in the kitchens, and there, under the colored lights and the branches, well, Renatino has fallen in love. Her name is Mercedes, and Renatino is so well set up that he can even screw her. He has only to put two men outside the door of his cell armed with machetes and guns to get all the peace you need for that sort of thing. Every other evening, more or less.

And every evening at about half past six or seven the show begins: the convicts fire up at the guards and the guards fire down at them. Now and again someone ends up on the morning wheelbarrow and leaves. For good. Nobody will even know who he was.

One evening a more violent quarrel than usual breaks out, a hail of lead between the tower and the yard. Renatino finds himself right in the middle and runs toward the guards with the intention of hiding in the library. But he doesn't make it. With him are his two Italian friends, and there's nothing for it but to throw themselves on the ground and pray. Instead of the angels of the Lord, however, it's the Guardia Nacional who arrive with an armored car and machine guns to wipe out sixty men in no time. It's a massacre, and the result is they take away all the weapons. Normality returns. But it's a rather tense normality. It's clear to Renatino by now that staying there a long time means a 70 to 80 percent chance of a short life. After only four years, mainly thanks to Mercedes, he gets a more liberal regime because of a new job, far more prestigious than his former one in the library: superintendent of hens on a prison farm (a Venezuelan prison is among other things a kind of business, with many partners and cheap labor). He moves to the farm. There he has a cottage all to himself. He starts breeding chickens, works hard at it with dedication, and soon has the business up and running. Before long he is able to supply fifty hens on request. He's practically a free man—a lot freer than his chickens, anyway. He has only another five years to go of this life. Renatino knows very well that the prison system in Venezuela is too small to cope with the numbers that pass through it. One Venezuelan in two spends a few years behind bars, but everyone gets kicked out halfway through his sentence to make room for the others. I was unlucky: if I'd been caught down there, I'd have been out so long ago that I'd already be inside somewhere else.

Meanwhile, Chávez has come to power, and Renatino, in deference to the government, passes himself off as an intellectual. In between his chicken breeding he starts giving classes. He teaches Venezuelan literature to the inmates. Some of them call him professor; he writes, eats well, has a good life. But freedom is worse than cocaine. As soon as you have some, it's never enough. So what does Renatino do? He leaves. Simple as that. He opens the door and leaves. That's how you escape in those parts, if you're wealthy enough to be a superintendent of hens. If you're not, there are other methods. For example, about eighty prisoners tunneled their way out. Renatino doesn't need to dig. He gets on a coach and returns to Cúcuta. And there he gets on another coach and goes to Bogotá. To the Italian embassy. To lay claim to an old sentence of four and a half years that is still outstanding at home: false invoices to the tune of ten billion lire. Yes, one of his previous activities had been selling plastic pipes. So he turns himself in and asks to be deported to Italy. They put him on the first plane out, which is a Lufthansa flight bound for Frankfurt.

In Frankfurt he is arrested by the German police, who take him before a judge for the preliminary hearing, and Renatino tells him the whole story. He doesn't know it, but he's had a stroke of luck: three German citizens have just died, burned alive in a Venezuelan prison. The judge is moved to think how hard life must have been for Renatino during all those years spent in that tropical hell down there in the Third World. "Before I send you to Italy," he says, "I'm going to let you rest for a while." He must have thought Renatino deserved it. He holds him for three months in a dream prison, as only the Germans make them. They have jam, a choice of various kinds of bread, a supermarket, windows made of bulletproof glass, and no bars, your cell key in your hand, gardens. Renatino thinks, This is Europe!

But it's not. It was only the gift of a German judge who pitied him his Venezuelan sufferings.

Three months, and the extradition order arrives. They whisk him off to Italy, to a prison not far from Busto Arsizio, which, if hell on earth exists, is it: bars, padlocks, and bolts everywhere, a smell of rot and intimidation, and strict discipline, two hours' recreation, gates, no interviews, so dirty you want to cry or vomit, disgusting food, and the smell of rancid soup that seeps right into your bones. On top of that, the supervising magistrate, a little man who introduces himself like this: "If you wish, you can file a complaint against me; it's your right. I have eight hundred complaints outstanding against me, but one thing is certain: you'll never get out of here." Renatino is in despair, suffocated, buried. Oh yes, here the problem is called "security." The prison guarantees your security and to this end deprives you of everything: air, light, hygiene. It keeps you locked up so that you (perhaps) won't get killed. What good are five years of security to me? he thinks. In Venezuela you give the warder a few dollars and you get meals brought from the restaurant. Do they try to poison the meals? It's better than this daily poison here. Aseptic? Certainly not! Asensory, more like. But filthy. That's the paradox of Italian prisons.

So what does Renatino do? He tries playing the culture card again, enrolls at a university, obtains a transfer to a quieter section, waits for the "little pardon," fills out the "little request," saves on the "little permit," runs the whole gamut of the self-contradicting diminutives of the Italian prison service, puts up with the dirt, puts down a deposit on a yacht in Venezuela. And as soon as he gets out, he disappears. Under Chávez's regime a pardon now costs ten thousand dollars, and our friend has already booked it. Ah, lucky man.

Throwing the Dogs Off the Scent

Even the small pushers sometimes enjoy putting one over on the authorities. They too like an act of daring from time to time, though they're usually pretty cowardly types. The difference between the mule and the *sistemista* isn't just in the head, it's in the guts too. Improvising is often a matter of courage as well as imagination. To show you the difference, I'll tell you how a *sistemista* once coped with the kind of situation that mules constantly have to face. The *sistemista* in question was yours truly. One day Oscar calls me on the telephone, in despair. He's got some debts; he needs money. The message is clear. He wants some cocaine to sell so that he can pay some cutthroat who's got him by the balls. I call Miguel in Miami:

"Listen, I've got a *coño* here who's giving me a lot of *mala vida*. I can't *tocar mi roba!* Couldn't you send me half a kilo so I can get him off my back?" Miguel is a good friend. He comes in person. We go to meet him at Hamburg airport, and I'd recognize him even if I'd never seen him before. Miguel is the guy in the snakeskin Texan boots worth six hundred dollars at the time. He takes out the insole, and the heel contains a little pad of cocaine, say 250 grams in each boot. The trouble is, he was too sure of himself and hadn't protected it. Okay, he arrives and we go to eat together. He's planning to leave the next day. But Oscar and I are wearing tennis shoes (oh, those shoes . . .). Where the hell are we going to put the merchandise? We think about it, and while we're thinking, I notice Oscar's big feet: he takes a 45, and with a bit of work it can be done. The stuff will fit under the insole. Except at the Brenner Pass there are dogs, and they're not Caribbean dogs.

One thing that should be said about dogs: there are many ways of fooling them. The most widely used distractor is coffee, and then there's cayenne pepper. Country people like garlic, which has the advantage of its very evocative aroma. You smell of garlic; therefore you're a harmless yokel who eats junk food on the street, not a courier. But the best products are the petroleum derivatives. I've always preferred engine grease. The important thing is never to make the mistake of using irritants (some people even use an antirape spray), because that drives the dog crazy, and a dog behaving strangely, if the guard isn't a complete idiot, will arouse suspicions. In any case, back home it's not unusual for a good narco to be on personal terms with the dog that sniffs his shipments. I've told you we often supply the dogs to the police. But there's more. When you prepare a shipment to be taken by couriers, obviously you do some tests on the protection, using dogs just like the ones you see in the airports. Guess who lends the smugglers the dogs they do the tests with? Easy, isn't it? Let's just say the German shepherd dogs of the South American police forces often do long stints, well rewarded with steak, on the coca farms and *cocinas*, testing whether their shipments are completely odorless.

As soon as we emerge from the pass and see them eagerly sniffing everything that moves, Oscar starts sweating, in a panic. But you can't stop. When you come out of the tunnel and see them right in front of you, there's nothing you can do. I know guys like Oscar. They snort to boost their courage, and then when they're high, they panic and go crazy. So I take off his shoes, pull out the insoles, and put the cocaine into McDonald's bags, to make it look as if there are hamburgers inside them. I keep hold of a couple of bags myself and hand the others to Oscar and two other guys who are in the back of the car. Disaster is always lying in wait, and that idiot of a partner of mine, in trying to get out of the car with his bag, tears it, and the cocaine spills out. Just as the customs men reach us.

"Where have you come from?"

"Hamburg."

"Documents, please?"

"Are we going to be here for a while? D'you mind if I get out, then, to stretch my legs?"

"Sure."

I get out clutching my two little bags, with the dog's nose less than ten yards away. A diversion is called for, so I take the sachet of ketchup and sprinkle it all over the bag. The dog comes closer, and I see him scent something. He's excited. Meanwhile the customs officials tell the others to get out of the car, and the dog goes in, gets excited—very excited—but doesn't find anything. He doesn't smell my stuff: dogs are stupid, and that one was crazy for a hamburger. Luckily, the customs official looks stern and says, "Have you been snorting during the journey? What have you been doing, smoking a joint?" But he soon loses interest and waves us on. At the first Motta service station we come to, we have to stop because Oscar has shit himself. Now, on that occasion I had to improvise, and I only had ketchup, but should you find yourself in that kind of situation, remember that mustard is much better—a wonderful dog distractor.

Come to think of it, that might be an idea for a new system . . . Now, where do they make good mustard? Ah, never mind . . .

LESSON THREE: Continental Transportation

Once upon a Time in Cuba

In the days of the small-scale systems, the center of everything was Cuba. It was always an important outlet, ideal for access to the United States, but also a stopping-off place for the suitcase and ovule merchants. It's an embarrassing fact for some, but the Disneyland of communism owes a lot to the work of people like me. The *Líder Máximo*, the "Great Leader," is quite open about it: drug smuggling is just another way of exploiting the contradictions of the corrupt North and using them against it. Cuba's a handy place. Everyone thinks people go there for the whores, not for cocaine. Castro has been lucky. The whores cover up the cocaine. In fact, international politics has never been a problem for business in the Gulf of Mexico. It's true that there's a continual war between Castro and the exile community in Miami, but on the other hand, Cuba is the ideal showcase for cash-strapped communism. Nobody's ever going to want to found another Communist state as long as this great open-air brothel exists only a stone's throw away from the American coast. You can rest assured that the United States will remain politically and culturally hands off and won't make any more mistakes like the Bay of Pigs anytime soon. Besides, even when Castro was a young Catholic boy, he was well known at the University of Miami because of the marijuana he sold.

When we used to go there, our motto was *Vamos al país de la maravilla!* We took plenty of dollars. The Cubans aren't stupid; they're not interested in pesos or other Latin *dinero*. We used to go up from Barranquilla, Colombia, in fast Cigarette boats, or from Mexico. Or else from Kingston, Jamaica. Cuba has long been an ideal staging post on the way to Europe. What you needed was a nice convenient group of tourists, the kind who come over from Italy, Spain, and France, with someone among them who was prepared to switch suitcases. The Italians are best; they come for a screw and go home with a wife. You prepare the Samsonites for them—not with the little cakes. This time you make a thin sheet of coca paste and line the inside of the suitcase with it. Allowing for the space occupied by the protective layers—the usual ones, grease and carbon paper—the amount you can pack in is exactly three kilos: half on top and half at the bottom. All you have to do is bring your Samsonite, pick up your load, and contact the courier: "Nobody will take any notice of you. You wash, comb your hair, and put on a tie, take these three thousand dollars (half will go to your family), and fly to Malpensa . . ." All easy, pleasant, as smooth as silk. That's *el paraíso del pueblo* for you. The checks on the way out of Europe are nonexistent (which makes this a good channel for money too), and even on the way in they're pretty perfunctory, especially for package tours. If the suitcase is lost, that might be a problem—in fact, that's how the package tour ruse came to an end. But sooner or later these things start up again, in waves.

Whenever they called me to come up from Barranquilla for a bit of spiced-up tourism, I always dashed to Havana, as happy as a baby. It's a joy. While the Beast of Birán delivers eight- or ten-hour political speeches and the loudspeakers blare, the Italians, who love their myths, kneel down in worship before him, and the children cluster around you. *Un dolarcito señor, por favor. Vienes tu de Italia? Y dónde están los dólares?* We were the smart guys from Barranquilla, do-it-yourself tourists with a little something extra. We used to meet at the Luna Negra, an old pirates' place in La Víbora. Small squares surrounded by shabby houses with zinc roofs. The whole place is bare, painted red, ocher, and white; there's a big fan on the ceiling and an old fortune-teller selling cigars.

The old fortune-teller is essential: before every operation the true narco goes to see the *santera*.

"Cómo será el viaje?" How will the journey go?

"Un éxito total!" It'll be a complete success!

And you pay her for this good news in advance. She doesn't cost much. What does cost you is the *impuesto*, the residence tax that supports the cartels.

I know, nobody likes talking cynically about a utopia, or even about the detritus of a better age that no longer exists, but if there's one thing I've learned while working my way around the world, it's that nobody turns up his nose at coca, especially when there's a guerrilla war being fought. There are no fine feelings when a rifle does the talking. My friend Alfonso used to travel around southern Mexico with his trailer packed full: a hundred kilos. Four jerks in camouflage gear stopped him and found the stuff: "We won't shoot you, but you've got to give us a contribution for the cause." He got off lightly: one kilo. That's how it works, even where they don't do colossal deals in the manner of the FARC.

In any case, Castro keeps a cool three million dollars in Switzerland. Where do you think that came from? Communist solidarity? The *revolución* is financed with the proceeds from the merchandise that financed the Contras who were fighting Ortega in Nicaragua. The stuff has no smell, nor does the money that comes from it. Even when it costs you a trusted comrade. Like Colonel Ochoa, the hero of the war in Angola and Namibia, an awkward customer, the kind of man who risks becoming a symbol and overshadowing the boss.

To get rid of him, they sent him to get himself killed along-side the leaders of the MPLA in Angola, along with another thirty thousand pieces of Cuban cannon fodder. But Ochoa made the mistake of coming back. The U.S.S.R. wasn't getting a ruble from Fidel, and what's more, they had to maintain him. The currency of exchange, at that time, was the Cuban soldiers used for dirty jobs over half the world, or at least half of Africa: Somalia, Mozambique, Angola. Ochoa had held his head high for twenty years. Having returned from Africa, and undefeated at that, he would eventually have become a threat. Besides, for some time the American State Department had been accusing the Cuban revolution of using cocaine to undermine the youth of North America. Nobody believed it, of course. The people who made the big money out of the merchandise that passed through Cuba worked for the department, enterprising officials of the CIA or FBI, policemen. But the myth of the corruptible youth of America suited both sides—the Yankees because it scandalized parents and kept things hot for Castro; Castro be-cause it provided a revolutionary and anti-imperialistic justifi-cation for his business dealings, which were so extensive and conspicuous that they couldn't be completely hidden from everyone. Often the genius of the great narco trafficker (or the great *líder*) takes the form of "two birds with one stone" or even "three birds with one stone." And so Ochoa was accused of, among other things, drug smuggling.

It's no coincidence that the Ochoa scandal broke immediately after the U.S. invasion of Panama to depose "pineapple face" Noriega, the man who made the fortune of those headline writers who invented the word "narco-dictator" and who is now rotting in a cell of some North American maximum-security prison. After the invasion, which enabled the Yankees to eliminate a man who was getting above himself, cocaine officially became, before the eyes of the whole world, the surest way of ruining someone politically. You create trouble? We put a ton of cocaine under your ass; then we send in the marines and receive the blessing that the world always bestows on heroes who combat the supreme evil. Ultimately, Castro, in nailing Ochoa, had simply applied the American lesson.

Yes, the great power of cocaine. What makes it lucrative even for those who combat it is its symbolic value: the absolute evil, the alien—what the Communist and the Martian used to be and what perhaps the Muslim is today. This symbolic value makes any punitive action permissible, and you have only to take up arms against cocaine to become the white knight. What is a *"Coronamos!"*—the cry of relief, joy, and mockery with which the great narco seals a successful venture— compared to a "Here come the marines" broadcast live on TV around the world, which cocaine can be relied on to provoke whenever it's needed.

Let's be quite clear: Castro is an anomaly, and the combination of statesman and drug lord that he embodied is possible only in Cuba and only in an age that's coming to an end. As the death of Escobar shows us, coexistence with political power is wiser than an attempt to usurp it.

The Third Cartel

It's widely believed that the big cartels no longer exist after the fragmentation of the 1990s. That's only partly true. One cartel does still exist, the third largest, a very interesting one that wasn't taken all that seriously until the European cocaine route turned out to be the salvation of the whole market. Take note of the third cartel: although it's the least known, it's crucial to the axis that brings business to Europe, and for various reasons it's almost untouchable. The organization's heart is the mountain forest, a no-man's-land on the border between Venezuela and Colombia to the west of Maracaibo, the lagoon, the pirates, and the Indians. This region is the Sierra Guajira, and it's swarming with all kinds of groups: FARC guerrillas, Nazi paramilitaries, smugglers, cutthroats, and agents in the pay of the North Americans or the Colombian government who are hoping to eliminate Chávez. But the Guajira is not controlled by the Yankees or by the Colombian government; it's controlled by a different group.

It's time to talk about Indians. In this region the cartel is an almost entirely Indian organization—less visible and based in areas regulated by an autonomous tribal law, with its own institutions, its own methods, its own codified relationships between extended families, incomprehensible to anyone who wasn't born in the forest. We mustn't speak ill of minorities, must we, and after five hundred years of extermination, it's not fair to blame the Indians, is it? It's not done to attack the victims. And yet the victims have to cope with their marginalization, and the narcos know that only too well. The NGOs thrive on minorities; if you blacken an Indian's reputation, you might derail one of their gravy trains. So let's get this straight. They're all very nice people, the terra-cotta faces, okay? Let's talk about my favorites: the Guajiros. They used to produce the best marijuana in the world, but coca was what made them real money. And since the upheavals of the 1990s, if you want to make money too—big money—they're the people to work with. They know what they're doing. It's foolish to underestimate them, yet people do underestimate them, especially the people who paint an idealistic picture of them.

Just one fact: no Indian has ever died because of cocaine. That happens only in the so-called West.

The Guajira cartel is still alive and flourishing today. It continues and it prospers, and it does so because it doesn't bother anyone else. It has a low, unthreatening profile because of its coexistence with the "clean" powers. Basically, the Guajiros know they're criminals and don't try to be anything else. That's the best policy. Previously their leader was "the Apache," the founder, a complete nut who liked spreading terror. Then in the 1980s there was a guy from Naples who married the princess of the Guajiros. He brought his know-how with him and diversified the business, producing prime marijuana and coca and supplying the fuel for Escobar's F-16. They called him the Prince because of his wife. He could get you anything, even an atomic bomb if you wanted one. He had a vineyard at Campo Mara. He took the stuff from Maracaibo to the area around Coro, where the big refineries are.

So the Guajira has had its romantic periods, but today the boss of the last big cartel is a great entrepreneur who owns planes and granary ships and does very good business with the guerrillas. The FARC has a force of twenty thousand armed men to maintain, and if you add their families, that makes a total of a hundred thousand people. Chávez regards them as a buffer against invasion from the west. Do you think they survive on handouts? But the cartel does good business with the paramilitaries too, who are the most dangerous people. There's no distinction on the market: you sell to the highest bidder, then let them fight it out between themselves. Those are people you can't avoid when you do this job. When I worked in the area around Huaychao in Peru, I had to deal with the Shining Path. They used to demand fifty dollars for every block of marble I transported (I'll explain later . . .). These are sums that add to your expenses; they're sustainable, though, if you cover them with the kind of profits you get from cocaine.

The Guajira cartel also has the advantage of being less interesting to the United States. It has less impact on public opinion, is less telegenic, less useful when it comes to internal politics. Until the collapse of Cali and Medellín, its main shipments didn't go to the North American coasts but were focused entirely on the West Indies and Cuba, especially as a jumping-off point for Europe. The Guajira was the biggest supplier to Cuba; the crucial point of entry was an airstrip on what was then Isla de Pinos, now called Isla de la Juventud. But Cuba is not an easy partner. It can be risky dealing with a country where control is so centralized. If the leader turns against you, your business will collapse. The Guajiros realized very early on that they needed to diversify.

And so, partly because of the new markets and the decline in the role of the United States, and partly because of the new organizational needs arising from the collapse of the two biggest Colombian cartels, at the beginning of the last decade a new road opens up: the South Road. Caribbean coca starts to move toward Brazil, Argentina, and Uruguay. The northward passage toward the United States and Canada—and from there, in smaller quantities, toward Europe—seems more and more tightly controlled and less and less remunerative. Europe, however, is asking for more and more merchandise, and supplying it becomes a matter of survival for the traffickers. So the road to the Old Continent snakes down to the south, and the cocaine seeks out new harbors, crossing the Andes, the forests, and the llanos to reach the ports of Rio, São Paolo, and Montevideo. The market changes, and the way the traffickers control it changes too. The need to secure the transit routes to the south and to the ports that send the big ships to Europe changes all the methods, the areas that have to be controlled, and the places where the money laundering is done. Even the migrant communities change. For example, the Triple Frontier, the paradise of the Iguaçu Falls on the border between Argentina, Paraguay, and Brazil, is transformed almost overnight into a new Tortuga, inhabited by us, the Lebanese, Asians, Orientals, and profiteers of every description.

Of course, it didn't take the DEA long to get wise to the new trail, and when the shipments on the South Road became significant, we had to use a bit of ingenuity. Only one country is "cold" as far as the CIA is concerned: Chile. It isn't closely watched, because internal transportation is very difficult—there's really only one road from north to south—and it has ports only on the Pacific, so it doesn't seem relevant to the European routes. And it doesn't produce a milligram of coca. So what did I do? I turned my attention to Chile. For a thousand dollars a kilo a friend of mine would carry the stuff for me on his trucks to Antofagasta from almost anywhere in South America. And that was the start of the great adventure of the darkness. The philosopher's stone.

The South Road opened up new perspectives and created a new kind of operator. First of all, the merchandise had to be moved within the continent. Coca wasn't produced everywhere, and above all it wasn't produced close to intercontinental harbors and airports. It was grown in Bolivia, Colombian Amazonia, and, to a lesser extent, Peru, Ecuador, and the extreme north of Argentina. So it had to be moved, mainly overland, to places from which it could be sent overseas. Soon, long caravans of trucks packed with incredible amounts of drugs made their way to ports that seemed above suspicion, where the merchandise could be carefully hidden and dispatched to Europe. One of the main highways for this flourishing trade was the Brazilian region of the Pantanal, chosen because it was central, impossible to control, and ideal for dispatching goods in any direction. In the late twentieth century the king of this kind of transportation was an Italian by the name of Bonazzi. A man whose story needs to be told.

An Italian on the South Road

Bonazzi merits a digression from our program of study. He's a trailblazer to the south, but above all he embodies to perfection the lifestyle of the people who smuggle cocaine. He has all the possible characteristics of the narco. And he's Italian too.

Height: five foot five; desire to work: zero. As squat as a wine flask, hewn out of a single block, two gorilla-like arms that reached down to his knees, nearsighted, likable; you couldn't help rolling about in laughter with him. His pride and joy was his penis. He used to show it to everyone. "John Holmes wanks this cock!" He was liable to greet you like that even if you didn't know him, and you should have seen the faces of certain ladies or of prissy male clients so desperate not to lose the deal that they were prepared to put up with it and pretend to find it funny. You should have seen them when he pulled out his tool and started talking: "When I take a shower and I want to clean it, first I have to lay it down on a tile and leave it there to wait for me while I wash the rest of my body. Then when I've finished, I scrub it down with a mule brush."

Bonazzi's a guy who'd caught the clap fourteen times. Fourteen claps in one lifetime! He still had his Apennine accent: he'd left Reggio Emilia just after the Second World War and emigrated to the United States—as so many people did at the time—confident that he was going to make his fortune, maybe in Los Angeles. A show-off right from the start, though he worked as a gardener. He knew how to get himself noticed, and soon he *was* noticed by one of Tony Spampanato's men. Spampanato was the guy who ran the catch circuit in the postwar years. You know what catch is? Fighting in fancy dress: wrestling, they call it nowadays. It was all faked, but back then, there was still the occasional gullible idiot who didn't realize the matches were fixed. Bonazzi had the right physique, and on top of that he had stamina and the will to succeed. He took up wrestling. In catch, each wrestler has to dress up as an archetypal figure—a tiger, say, or an escaped convict—so Bonazzi played a Venetian Harlequin. He had a special costume made for him. He used to swear a bit under his mask and swing his fists about. Incredibly, the character was popular, and Bonazzi's career prospered. His ready tongue proved an asset too; he started hanging around with people like Sam Giancana, the boss of bosses, and naturally, he started to think he was something special. He traveled around with the catch circus, made new friends, and often worked in Las Vegas, so things were going well for him until one day he was called in by the FBI. They labeled him "persona non grata," whether because of the people he hung out with or on some other more specific charge, I don't know—he would never say—but the fact is, they didn't mess about in those days. Non grata, and that was that. If you weren't wanted, you left. Period. But you could choose where to leave to, and Bonazzi chose Venezuela.

He didn't stay long; the country didn't appeal to him. It happens. Two lovers who don't hit it off at their first meeting. So Bonazzi went back to Italy, and then, almost immediately, left again. This time for Brazil. His plan was to set up a catch company in Rio or São Paolo and get back into business. But nobody was interested in costumed wrestlers down there, or maybe Bonazzi just hadn't yet developed that entrepreneurial spirit that would make him his fortune later on. At any rate, the plan failed. So he thought of putting his oversize penis to remunerative use. He started working as a gigolo, but since he was as ugly as a macaque's ass, he got very little money for his pains and a lot of beatings. A hell of a life. But he made friends with Italians, lots of Italians, rich Italians—more and richer Italians than he'd ever imagined he would find in those parts. Making friends is always a useful and profitable activity, especially for a future maestro like Bonazzi. Among the maestros *he* learned from was a guy from Vicenza who later made a fortune building villas in Spain but at that time transported fruit from Bolivia—and incidentally, of course, cocaine concealed under the floors of the trucks—breaking his journey in the Pantanal, where he stopped to pay off the Indian workers whom he had brought across from the other side of the border. The Pantanal was an important lesson for Bonazzi. It was there that our friend learned a method that was both safe and well suited to exportation, a method by which he was to prosper for a long time. Lead.

Actually, it's a method that's probably been around for centuries—at least since the invention of gunpowder. But for convenience's sake we can date it to the early 1970s and locate it in the Pantanal of Rondônia, beyond the Mato Grosso Plateau, in that strip of borderland between Brazil and Bolivia that falls under the jurisdiction of São Bento on the Brazilian side and Estancia Reynoza on the Bolivian side. It's a floodplain between the Amazon River and Paraguay: muddy tableland as far as the eye can see, and a road that crosses the border and skirts the swamps. For long periods of the year the road is impassable because it's underwater. When it emerged, it was used by the big trucks that carry cocaine from Bolivia: special tractor-trailors with very high sides. The maize was loaded on, 2,200 pounds per vehicle. Most of them were North American Macks—indestructible bison, suited to the roughest of cart tracks, like the North Yungas Road, which rises from La Paz to some 15,000 feet at La Cumbre and then plunges vertiginously down to Coroico, at 3,900 feet, leaving at least one truck per week in the chasms that run alongside it. The most dangerous road in the world. But if the Macks, with their cargoes of maize, did get past that stretch, they then disappeared into the forest. Maize is bulky and needs those extra-high sides, so it was easy to create an extra ten centimeters at the bottom by laying down pallets. By feeding in bricks of coca paste tied together with string through the gap underneath, you could carry as much as a ton of coca in one convoy. Nobody checked the roads there, and the merchandise quietly made its way toward São Paolo. This guy from Vicenza, who was very active at least until 1985, had developed his own special method for loading the merchandise and getting it across the border.

Payment in Lead

His method was the campesinos. After the job was done, you took them out to eat, and especially to drink (he was no heartless butcher, he liked to give them a bit of pleasure before bumping them off), before taking them out rolling drunk into the swamp (soon it would be covered with water and full of hungry animals) and paying them off.

He paid them in bullets. His pupil Bonazzi over the next few years simply refined his method by hiring members of the Guardia Nacional to do the job—they were always up for a bit of well-paid, entertaining work and for taking part in the fiesta that invariably followed the payoff. But even payment in lead required a minimum of planning: for example, you really did give the peasants their money. But after massacring them, you took it back. You went and fished it out of their pockets and bags. And some of it stayed in the Guardias' uniforms. That meant more satisfaction all around and fewer problems for everyone. Don't get me wrong, the drug smugglers weren't the only ones to use this method. The big *fazendeiros* used it for a long time too, and maybe it's still used in some places. It works for the wholesale fruit business too. I'll never tire of repeating it: it's not the nature of the merchandise that creates the monster, it's the market. Diabolic substances are a fantasy of romantics and bankers. The stuff can be good or bad, just as an apple can be good or bad; a man can be bad, just as a dog can be bad. It's men who decide how they make use of the substances and the money. Not the other way around.

The cleaning up afterward was done by the anacondas and the crocodiles. In a very short time not a trace remained of the payoff.

So Bonazzi made his trips across the Pantanal, learning a lot, until one of the Italians told him about Venezuela. He said the people there had been crazy about Italians ever since the time of Pérez Jiménez, land was dirt cheap, and the president was giving it away like candy. Bonazzi gave Venezuela another try. He went back and bought himself a small plot of land, about seven hundred acres on the road from Perijá to Maracaibo, put some animals on it, and found that things began to work. And he imported the methods he'd learned on his travels around the world. It takes more than a few thousand square miles of forest to stop proven methods and reliable organizational structures from catching on.

So the Venezuelan *fazendeiros* of Santa Barbara on the Río Limón, of the Guajira, the Sierra de Perijá, and the Sierra Nevada, all learned how to use lead. Bonazzi, a few years after his Brazilian apprenticeship, worked on the route between Maicao, in Colombia—north of Bogotá—and Ríohacha, on the Caribbean coast, and from there to Coro. Nasty road, that: the kind you travel along only with an armed escort, and what an escort! The place was full of bandits and Guajiro Indians who would slit your throat as soon as look at you. But it was worth all the effort. From Ríohacha and Santa Marta you could easily reach the Antilles with merchandise and money, though the sea crossing wasn't simple. It was patrolled, and it was rough, which is a problem even if you have a three-hundred-horsepower Cigarette, the boat most commonly used by the people who work in this business. But if, instead, you chose to head east overland through the forest and came out on the Maracaibo side, you could avoid the patrols and the heavy seas. There's nothing but desert up there, and sand dunes; and if you took a boat and headed north for San Francisco, on the tip of the Paraguaná Peninsula, skirting the eastern coast of the Gulf of Venezuela, where you had to slalom your way between the oil rigs, you found yourself only eighteen sea miles from Aruba. Even in the flimsiest of craft you could then easily get to Curaçao and Bonaire, or to Saint Kitts and Saint Martin, the safest area. Except that to reach Coro, you had to take the treacherous road that crosses the Venezuelan border at Santa Bárbara del Zulia. At the beginning of the last decade, the escorting, loading, unloading, and transporting was done by Guajiros employed by Bonazzi or by other entrepreneurs, all of European origin.

Recruiting the Indians wasn't difficult. They were starving. You picked them up early in the morning in the squares on the Colombian side of that nonexistent border. They did seasonal work—on coca, but above all, there too, on fruit, maize, and livestock, the Venezuelan milk cow. They'd do six months for you, eating and sleeping in the *fazenda*. Okay, toward the end of the season there was always someone who guessed what was going to happen and slipped away, but you could spot who was likely to do a runner, and they were isolated cases. The great thing about these tapioca eaters is that deep down they're extreme individualists. The entrepreneurs needed to take only one precaution: when you recruit, it's best to choose mainly single men, guys without families.

Yes, the ones with families sometimes survived.

A Curb on the Massacres

The game ended—officially, at least—in the 1980s, when the missionaries got involved. They were pretty astute, and amiable enough if you met them in the jungle and you weren't their objective. There was one of them, a Jesuit, on the Colombian side of the Guajira, who knew how to do his sums. He'd heard the words "I'm going to work in Venezuela" too often spoken by people who had subsequently vanished into thin air, and since he was an intelligent guy, he'd asked himself a few questions. You have to bear this in mind too: the forest has a million ears, and by this time strange stories were circulating in the villages and therefore in the churches too. This Jesuit, like all the inhabitants of the area, was deeply tanned from years of living in the sun, and he was also a thin, irascible guy, accustomed to working in the forest, so when he was dirty, he was indistinguishable from a Guajiro. And he spoke the dialects of the sierra like a native.

Well, the priest did his sums, had his suspicions, and decided to investigate. He knew he didn't need to change his appearance much; he just had to wash a bit less, grunt a bit more, and turn up early one morning in the square of some village in the interior, surrounded by clouds of dust that were the same color as his face. In the square he met Bonazzi's recruiters—who knows, maybe he even met Bonazzi himself. After all, my friend was an old-fashioned entrepreneur. There were some things he liked to do himself. Anyway, the priest was hired and crossed the border with the teams bound for the *fazendas* on the other side. "Now let's see what happens on the Venezuelan side . . ."

The problem for our intrepid Jesuit was that on Saturdays, Bonazzi was in the habit of loading all his victims onto a truck and taking them off to a brothel. He was thoughtful that way. And they, horny as monkeys, had got into the unfortunate habit of washing before they went. The missionary realized at once that if he joined them, and especially if he washed, he might be recognized. Rumors started going around the fields, and after a while everyone was talking about this strange guy who never washed and didn't go to the brothel, who kept to himself and always had a surly expression on his face. Bonazzi's supervisors began to suspect there was something wrong. They told the boss, he thought it over, and at the end of the season he decided to spare the workers. There was something fishy about this guy; better not to take any risks. Besides, Bonazzi possessed the narco's most important characteristic: he was creative. That year he introduced a new method, his own industrial makeover. He paid his campesinos with sick cows—infected animals as money—and sent them home, happy and convinced that they'd made a good deal and cheated the cheese-faced *musiú*. However, the priest wasn't stupid either; he realized that something funny must have happened. Payment in sick animals couldn't be the norm, unless there was an epidemic every season. He had a hunch. Back in his parish, he waited and prepared his next move.

He had a trusted assistant, a Guajiro sacristan, one of those parish mice who knows forty words more than the other campesinos and always finds a way of using them to his advantage. The Jesuit made the little guy a proposal he couldn't refuse. He sent the sacristan to take his place in the work party and this time made a careful note of the names of all the men who left for the border. The brothel was no problem for the sacristan, but it was clear that things had changed. Even the terra-cotta faces had twigged in the end; the rumors had multiplied, and fear was spreading. The sacristan was an intelligent guy and realized things might come to a head sooner than expected. There's nothing so dangerous as a cornered *musiú*. Apart from certain snakes, of course. So the boy decided to jump the gun, and he got out early, with a lot of harvesting still to be done. I don't know whether the priest whipped him or thanked him, but he too thought it was suspicious. He gathered a large troop of local elders (village chiefs and other ragamuffins, not particularly dangerous, but as persistent as swamp ticks) and rushed over the border to see what Bonazzi was doing. Too late. The sound of shotgun fire could already be heard from the woods. The slaughter had begun and was over almost immediately. Calling the local police wasn't likely to be of any use; they were sure to be on the payroll. It was obvious even to a Jesuit that a job like payment in lead couldn't be done without the connivance of the powers that be. But he tried all the same, thinking that the authority of the cassock might just force them to act. But no, they took their time, strung it out as long as possible, and probably snarled at the priest when he tried to hurry them up. Then they staged their raid. They knew perfectly well that the farm was full of their colleagues from the Guardia Nacional, busy slitting the throats of a few Indians to earn a bit of cash on the side. In their free time, like everybody else, they used to take their uniforms off and form squads of *matones* at the service of the landowners, paid piece rates, so much per *cabeza*—that is, according to the number they killed. So during the raid the cops in uniform recognized the cops in plain clothes, exchanged winks with them, and carried out a thorough inspection now that the killing was over, knowing full well that the survivors were so terrified that they usually had no inclination to report anyone. There were *matones* everywhere in the forest, and they might turn up at your home later, when you weren't there, to pay a little visit to your family.

Bonazzi and his men got away with it. But that was enough to put pepper on his ass. Now he was scared. All it would take was one politician in search of votes, or maybe a bishop, and he'd be in big trouble. A good entrepreneur knows when it's time for a change of tack, and you can say what you like about Bonazzi, but nobody could accuse him of not being a shrewd businessman. There were no prosecutions and no convictions, but the story was out now—manna from heaven for the journalists—and from that time onward payment with lead became more difficult, at least in the Guajira. What's more, in recent years a new wave of Italians had arrived in the country, and they tended to be less ruthless than their predecessors. A new era had begun—the age of the underpaid worker, the broken promise, sick animals on occasion, and the legal quibble. Less profitable than lead, certainly, but you could always find some way of fooling the Guajiros. Even though they too had learned to make frequent use of lawyers and rabble-rousers: political agitators, trade unionists, campesino leaders. Now, those guys really were worth killing, occasionally, but not the peasants anymore.

Bonazzi, Sex Trader

In any case, lead or no lead, before long Bonazzi had finally made his fortune. He set up a *fazenda* of at least fifty thousand acres, with three thousand *cabezas de ganado*—head of cattle, healthy ones. Sure, it's hard work running a farm like that, but in this kind of business he was no slacker. It didn't take him long to find a *querida*, and since he wasn't short of money and there were a few girls fluttering around him, he soon found a mistress too. In Venezuela, for some reason, the penis thing worked.

Subdivision of sex work among the Venezuelan narcos: the wife is the one who runs things back at home; the mistress is a gentleman's appurtenance. You keep her in town, pay for her apartment in the center, jewels, evenings at the theater, beautiful clothes, official dinners with the authorities, things like that. The *querida* is a more homey, less-demanding kind of lover. All you have to do for her is support her family, because there's always a family, and after all you are quite fond of her. Whores don't count. They're needed only when you're with friends or for business, and in fact there's no need for the wife to be too jealous of the *querida* either. The wife is still the lady of the house, she's the one who makes the decisions about the hacienda. And the good narco behaves toward her as he does toward the government: coexistence and no overlapping of roles. Bonazzi has a wife too, of course: Inés, a woman who says to him, "I only married you for your cock. I'm of Colombian origin." He replies, "That's fine with me. I'm Italian. I'm used to dealing with whores." So his wife suggests, "Let's set up a little business using hookers from Colombia. You test-drive them; then we can put them on the market." And that's how Bonazzi started importing from Colombia. At one stroke he and his wife set up their hacienda and their brothel: the O.K. Corral, the jewel in Bonazzi's crown.

For a while Inés's plan went well. Bonazzi went to fetch the girls from Colombia and tried them out, and the brothel—*tiradero* is the local term for it—proved a great success. But one day Inés discovered that she was jealous, as jealous as hell. Bonazzi used to tell it like this: "She had a special method for checking up on me. First she'd make me come; then she'd take the sperm and examine it. If she didn't like the consistency, she'd bash me over the head with a stick." They had five children. He, of course, also had his mistress, two *queridas*, and tasting rights when it came to the hookers.

By this time Bonazzi had a flourishing *tiradero*, his three thousand head of cattle, an immense *fazenda*, and at least fifteen hundred acres of wild woodland, which he used for hunting the *tigre*—the jaguar, that is—and the boa. And maybe also for paying off employees. Where do people go for sex? To the *tiradero*! Every narco either owns or manages one. Another word for it is *culiadero*. Bonazzi likes to be special and soon opens a second one. But although he had two, you would always find him at the O.K., his favorite. He had designed it himself. A *tiradero* is usually just a kind of warehouse divided up into compartments, makeshift bedrooms for people to have sex in, but he had planned the O.K. carefully to satisfy certain tastes of his own. He had created a room in the loft with a hole in the ceiling of every bedroom so that he could wank himself off at the punters' expense. His favorite phrase was *"Vamos a tomar un palito a mi tiradero!"*—Let's go and get laid in my whorehouse! I can see him now, with that broad, lustful grin of his. "I don't want to fuck your women! They're dirty!" I'd reply. We were always taking the piss out of each other. Oh, but I went there all right. Once, on the threshold of the O.K., we were welcomed by La Negra, the duty cashier at the time. She was Bonazzi's favorite. She would stand swaying in the doorway of the little waiting room, releasing a cloud of perfume that you could smell right out in the woods, with those great, wide hips that some women of the lagoon have. Then, when she saw you, she'd flash you a smile of dazzling quartz and disappear into the gloom, quick to get behind the cash desk. You know how it is: we're all friends, but unless it's on the house, payment is strictly in advance. Well, on that occasion Bonazzi arrived and didn't say a word. He liked to show off. An "It's on me" from Bonazzi could be heard almost as far away as Caracas. He would arrive with his chest puffed out, making great gestures with his arms, because he was that kind of guy; he liked to feel generous. But that day he didn't say a word. He entered quickly with us close behind, and La Negra, who evidently had a clear idea of her job description, dashed around to take up her post behind the cash desk. Now, I don't know if it's possible for a Negress to turn pale, but I'd swear she went as white as a sheet and screamed like a cat caught in a gin trap. I can see her now, shooting out from behind the counter and crashing into the arms of Bonazzi, who was laughing so much he could hardly support her. She had stepped on something soft and, since she wasn't used to its being there, had bent down to feel what was under the cash desk and found the little rug that Bonazzi had prepared for her: a boa as thick as a lady's muff, which he'd picked up and left there some time earlier for his own amusement. La Negra wouldn't stop screaming, so eventually Bonazzi took his rifle down from the wall and shot the boa. I think he still keeps it hung up somewhere around the house. His whole house was plastered with animal skins. At the age of sixty-five he'd become a landowner, and he wanted people to know it. The walls were covered with animal heads. The only heads he didn't have were Indian ones. But some rooms I never saw, and knowing him, I wouldn't be surprised if he had some of those too.

For him, whores were a passion, a trade, a vocation. One thing Bonazzi never learned, though, despite the years he spent up north, was English. Once, we were in Jamaica. We got off the plane at Kingston airport and were picked up in a yellow and blue taxi. Two-toned because it was made out of two different cars and held together with string. The driver tied the door to his elbow with a little rope so that he wouldn't lose it on the curves. Bonazzi really enjoyed that kind of thing: at every curve, of course, the door would swing open, and he'd shriek "Tek eet easy!" at the driver, but you could tell he was loving it.

We visited a small factory we were thinking of buying: a five-minute job. Afterward we went to the hotel. The Hilton, of course, as befitted a pair of successful businessmen. Before we'd even crossed the lobby, Bonazzi was poring over the yellow pages. "May I help you, sir?" says a big black flunky in a bow tie and a blue uniform, and Bonazzi asks him straight out: "Where eez the beetch?" Succinct but unequivocal. The doorman, however, at first misunderstands and thinks he's being asked for directions to the beach, but at a bark from Bonazzi he quickly understands and with impeccable manners prints out a list of addresses of the seediest brothels in Kingston. Bonazzi resolves to try them all. For him it was part of the business. He appraised whores as he did cows: he tested them, and if any seemed suitable, he offered them a job in his *tiraderos* in Venezuela.

He had his interracial side, did old Bonazzi. He had a passion for collective blow jobs given by three women of different ethnic groups, but his favorites were the Guajiros. They're women with ever-shining, wide eyes, and they have one peculiarity that makes them precious to the narco: their pussies are hairless and tight, and they come like elephants in heat, screaming and squirming so much you think you'll never get your cock out of there alive. "The day I can't get it up anymore," Bonazzi used to say, "I'm not going to give up sex! When that day comes, I'm going to get myself fucked in the ass. Well, I'll have to do something, won't I?"

He'd developed a passion for brothels, and he decided to set up another one on the Machiques-Colón road. And it was there that one day our successful businessman ran over a Guajiro. Relations with the Indians are always a problem in our part of the world.

Negotiations Guajiro Style

Listen to this. One bright afternoon—one of those afternoons when everything is white and the sky is indistinguishable from the lime-covered walls—Bonazzi is driving along the Machiques-Colón road in his clapped-out Fleetwood Cadillac. He was scary when he was at the wheel. He'd gesticulate, laugh, fool around, talk to you while looking you in the eye, and accelerate in fits and starts. If you hadn't vomited your guts out after half an hour, it meant you'd had a good trip. Well, the old crate is racing along between the rows of Guajiros who vegetate on the roadsides selling slices of goat meat, surrounded by buzzing flies and hungry iguanas. Their faces are all alike: a drowsy grimace and the whites of their eyes indistinguishable from the color of the sky and the walls. They sit there from dawn to dusk, twelve hours or more, selling their long strips of meat to passersby. Bonazzi is digesting, he feels terribly sleepy, he's practically dropping off at the wheel. He's just had a day, a night, and a day of work at the *tiradero* or in some even filthier place. The fact is, since these guys have the bad habit of stepping right out in front of you, waving their pieces of chewy meat, after a while either you stop to buy some or you try to get rid of them by stepping on the gas. Bonazzi chooses the latter option but makes a mistake: he veers off course, hears a shout and a bang, stops, and realizes he's in trouble. Under his wheel lies an eminent Guajiro with a broken leg, whimpering and showering him with insults.

Bonazzi was completely devoid of morality, and since he always kept a submachine gun—an Uzi—in his Fleetwood, his first thought with regard to the crippled Indian was, naturally enough, to finish him off and hide the body. There are limits to what the Guajiros will put up with. They have their own laws, and what's worse, the Venezuelan state, in the end, does give them a bit of protection. The Sierra de Perijá is a fickle region. It changes like a shadow with the passing of the sun. Everything is sand and flies up into the air at the first breath of wind, and as if that weren't enough, the Indians all have dual citizenship: Venezuelan and Colombian. The only things they've taken from civilization are alcohol, robbery, and a dual passport. And on the Perijá line they're the bosses. On the Colombian side there are three groups of Guajiros that support the guerrillas and one that supports the paramilitaries. They have their own laws and plenty of weapons, so they feel invincible. They control Maicao, to the south, the largest black market in the world. Down there either you know people or you don't know people. If you don't know people, you're dead. In the Río Limón area where Bonazzi used to make his "payments," on the straight and endless road to Ríohacha and Santa Marta, you'll just disappear. So the state might as well accept the sovereignty of the tribes' law, the *ley guajira,* which enjoys full recognition in those parts; and as if by magic, an ordinary, stinking cacique brushes the cloud of mosquitoes away from his fringe and becomes a judge recognized by the state. A disaster.

While Bonazzi is doing his calculations, all the Indians of the forest leap out of the trees, as angry as crocodiles. His first reaction is again that of an old murderer: I'll shoot them all. Then he counts, realizes that there really are a lot of them, and has second thoughts. Better to negotiate. "I'll take you to the hospital."

The Guajiros are all called Hernández, Fernández, and Gutiérrez. Bonazzi finds all those howling Fernándezes and Gutiérrezes in front of him, all identical, with their flower-patterned tunics, their smelly sandals, and their little round faces with sparse beards and little hats on top. They walk in Indian file, smoke marijuana all day, and never eat. He knows quite a number of these perspiring Hernándezes: he has a hundred and fifty of them on the hacienda. They work from seven to eleven and from three to seven, and they're perpetually drunk. Hiring them is easy. You load them onto the back of your truck and then tip them out in the farmyard. Getting rid of them when the work is finished isn't difficult either. This is no longer the age of lead: Bonazzi pays them at the end of the week, and he knows that on Saturday, instead of a hundred and fifty, there'll be three thousand of them, because the women always come with the whole family to collect their pittance. They do this to prevent their husbands from spending it all on beer and whores by Sunday evening. "*Musiú*, give me the money first, then give me my husband," say those wise women with terra-cotta faces. They're ugly to look at, these Guajiros, but they work like devils, they make fantastic holes in a very short time; these are guys who could dig a new Panama Canal with their bare hands.

In short, it's dangerous to underestimate them. The Guajiros do precise sums. If an accident leaves a man unable to provide an income for his family, if he can't raise and sell his meat, for example, their law lays down a codified and rigid system of compensation. With one notable exception: for the *musiú*, the foreigner. Ah, for him, the whiteskin, it's much harsher! There's not much chance of a European harming a Guajiro and escaping punishment.

So, just because he scribbled a couple of words on a scrap of paper and, instead of reaching for his Uzi, gave it to the victim lying in the road, the upshot is that Bonazzi wakes up one morning and finds two coaches parked outside his front door. Teeming with savages. And what's more, a procession of carts laden with women, babes in arms, all kinds of junk, smoked meat, and bottles. They set up camp. They've come equipped for a party. He realizes that the negotiations are going to be protracted.

Protracted, not difficult. The Guajiro law is basically just the old idea of tit for tat. Sure enough, the first proposal is "We break your leg." The black-faced judge stares fixedly at him (I wonder how old he is, thinks Bonazzi. They're all the same, these drunks) and continues: "But we like cerveza, my friend. We're civilized people. Let's come up with some numbers." With the *musiú* they set the price high, and they set it in dollars, not bolívars. And, well, if you have sixty, seventy people stationed morning and evening outside your house eating, drinking, and crapping everywhere and wringing the necks of your chickens, you don't really have much room for maneuver. And Bonazzi has to work: the whores, for example, need an eye kept on them; otherwise some local operator is likely to come along and steal the most attractive ones. And then there's the problem of the livestock: if the workers don't see you on the farm for a while, they slaughter the cows on the spot and take them home. The boss needs to keep an eye on things if he's going to survive on the Perijá. Therefore he has to negotiate.

"He's young . . . He's the breadwinner . . . He's a hard worker . . . It will take him four, even five months to recover . . . They want ten thousand."

"Dollars?"

"Dollars."

"It's too much. I'd rather kill you all."

"It's a solution. But then other Guajiros will come and kill you."

"I'll give you five hundred."

This is where the real negotiations begin, in the local financial language.

"Hijo de puta." Son of a bitch.

"Coño de tu madre." Your mother's cunt.

"Recoño de tu avuela puta." Your grandmother's snatch.

"Maldita sea la reverga de tu hijo." A plague on your son's cock.

And a whole string of other similar pleasantries. The refined idiom of the Guajiros. It was the only thing about those stinkers (apart from their hairless pussies) that Bonazzi liked.

Two days of fierce argument. The broken man's mother weighs in too. He can't satisfy his wife anymore, he can't visit his mistress, his *querida* . . . These are things that have to be paid for.

The agreement is as follows: seven hundred dollars, and on top of that Bonazzi buys a goat from the victim's family. The one who takes the money, of course, as quick as a flash, is the wife, who does the accounts. With that money she can support the children for six or seven months, and she has three hundred dollars left over, which she gives to her husband, who that very same evening ensures that they're given straight back to Bonazzi by spending them at the whorehouse.

Bonazzi Goes Home

He was a smart guy, he always got away with it, but he was restless. And so, inevitably, the day comes when he is fed up with Indians and *queridas* and boa hunting. He decides to go back to Reggio Emilia. He hasn't got many relatives, but there must still be someone there. This was before Black Friday. It must have been 1992 or 1993, the bolívar was exchanging at 4.3 to the dollar, and for half a million bolívars you got more than a hundred thousand dollars. Bonazzi comes around to see me, says he needs a partner to help him sell the hacienda; he's taken one on but isn't happy. I tell him he'll have to keep his partner; business isn't going too well for me at the moment.

Barely twenty-four hours later Bonazzi turns up at the Hotel San José in Maracaibo, where I happen to be with my other friends of that time, and announces that he's going back to Italy. But let it be quite clear that he's not going to say a word about it to his wife, mistress, *querida*, children, or whores. Only to us.

"I'm going back to civilization for a while!"

He says goodbye and leaves. It's normal in Venezuela. That's what people do. You don't tell your family anything about your business affairs. They can't be accused of anything, and you don't get nagged.

And when the door of the San José opens, it's normal for everyone to start cursing because of the conditioned air coughing out and swirling around. With that old oil-fired boiler they used at the San José, cooling the heat was an undertaking that took weeks. But on this occasion the curses stick in our throats. Less than a month has passed since that tearful farewell, and Bonazzi is there again, standing in the doorway, as chunky as ever but a little more angry.

"It's shit."

"What's shit?"

"Reggio Emilia."

"Oh, come on, Bonazzi!"

"It's shit in winter anyway, believe me. It's freezing . . . I arrived in my light flowery jacket, do you understand? I've hardly stepped off the train and I have to spend a million lire on a new overcoat."

"Never mind, old friend, at least you've got a new wardrobe . . . Italian shoes . . ."

"Italian shoes? Seven hundred thousand lire a pair! For that money over here I could buy two Guajiro slave girls and put *them* on my feet."

"What about your friends?"

"I turn up at home and they give me a warm welcome, sure! But it doesn't last long. On the second day my brothers send me to a hotel. 'After all, you can afford it, can't you?'"

"Huh, families . . ."

"On the third day I go looking for something to screw, but I've grown old. No woman will even look at me. So I decide to go looking for whores, in the evening out on the ring road. Even the whores won't look at me. Only an old one who wants three hundred thousand lire for a fuck. And she's as ugly as sin."

"Did you pay up?"

"Did I, hell! I ended up wanking off in a porn cinema. Seven days, and I was already sick of this lousy Reggio Emilia. I rush around to the travel agency. And there they tell me I can't leave: I've got a thirty-five-day ticket . . . I'm never going back to Italy again. My God, never again! I phone my wife and my *querida*: 'Get your legs wide open, because when I get home, I'm going to shag you stupid!' Shag you stupid, my ass! Twenty days' wanking I had to do before I could get out of there. I'm sick of civilized countries!"

After two days in Maracaibo, Bonazzi was again like a mouse in the cheese. "I'm a benefactor here," he liked to say, though he amused himself by shooting his Guajiro workers, the "sparrows of the Río Limón," as he called them. He sets up another brothel with holes in the ceiling and resumes his old life. By the mid-1990s he no longer had his mistress. He'd sold the hacienda and bought himself a luxury apartment in the middle of Maracaibo. He lived there with his whores from the O.K., and in the evening he would go down to the San José to tell his stories. I don't know about his wife. The concept of the family in those parts is pretty random. Of course, that's not the morality of the hidalgos, the 10 percent of families called Mendoza or Cisneros who control everything and strut around like great gentlemen. Those guys have wives, children, hearths, and trophies and fly around in helicopters. And they rule the roost. Always. But the average Venezuelan is, as I've told you, a whoremonger. The same goes for the Venezuelanized foreigner. The ethos is summed up in a favorite saying of Bonazzi's: *"Viejo y sin plata vuelves a mierda."* Old and penniless, you return to what you were. The rest passes.

A Table of Rogues

They were good times, the days of the South Road. I had settled in Venezuela, and when I wasn't working, I liked to lounge at the Italians' table in the San José. *Grand Hotel* San José, to give it its full title: bedbugs, mosquitoes, insects everywhere, and the worst of them were sitting around my table of rogues. I liked everything about that world, even the soup at ten bolívars, cockroaches included, that old Pinton, the owner, used to make. Everything eternally shrouded in the warm wind that takes hold of you, along with the boredom. Fantasies, excesses. It never rains, never. Men, animals, trees, as dry as the wood of a mandolin. If you want drinking water, you have to use a desalinator. Now and then, to get the dried dung off us, we'd escape to the Hyatt Regency on Aruba to enjoy a bit of the high life. There was also this village at about 6,000 feet, Colonia Tovar, about forty miles from Caracas. A clear, fast road, and by magic you find yourself in Germany. Every one of the villagers a Nazi, eh? But there were cherries! In Venezuela! It was marvelous to go and have breakfast there under the open tents in front of the little church with its white, European-style belfry. I used to go there with Sisto Da Re, the gigantic bullshit artist.

Sitting around the table there was usually me, Bonazzi, Sisto, Captain Leonardi, a Sicilian irredentist, and Michel, a French pilot who was later decapitated at Palito Blanco. They called me Piastrella, "Tile," because of my official job—marble—and at the table I nearly always sat next to the emperor of liars, Da Re of Montebelluna. And toward the end of the meal old Pinton himself would come and sit down with us, invariably with a cigarette in his mouth. He died of cancer, of course.

It was our refuge, a place reserved for us; if someone else was sitting there, old Pinton would make him get up and go and scratch off his ticks somewhere else. He'd cook for us personally. It was a dump, but there was lasagna: on Sundays the people would queue up for a takeout meal. The pasta was made by Michele, the cook, who drank himself to death. Old Pinton? How can I describe him to you? You know Andy Capp? The spitting image, minus the scarf. In his hotel you could live it up for very little money: three bolívars for a meal, and if you were Italian, he would sometimes treat you.

"Pinton, dame doble!" Hey, Pinton, bring me a double portion!

"Cómo no, Pablito!" Sure, Pablito!

He'd bring a normal portion and cut it in half.

"Aquí es el doble!" There's your double portion!

He hailed from Conegliano, up in the Veneto; his favorite interjection was "Are you mad?" in dialect: *"Sis tu mat?"* All the other Italians in our group thought he was talking about Sisto. Ignorant southerners.

Sisto had started by putting his diploma as a land surveyor to good use in a great job in the Guasare, the largest coalfield in

Venezuela. He did surveys and made 130,000 dollars simply by haggling over the price—a hell of a lot of money at the time. It was 1970. Now he could set himself up, so he put his diploma away and became a trader. Well, I say trader . . . Mainly he got by on the money he'd earned and told a pack of lies about it on the phone to Italy. He bought emeralds in Bogotá and took them to Italy. Most people there had never seen emeralds before, and when they held one in their hands, they never knew whether it was genuine. Those were golden years for exporting from South America. You could sell helicopters, really big things. Sisto didn't want to be outdone. He usually said he dealt in bamboo, but I don't think he ever saw even a sample of the stuff. So it came naturally to him to make up another story like the one about the two containers; it didn't even occur to him that people might not believe him. "*Do* containers," he'd say, and he'd hold up two fingers.

"Hey, Piastrella, do you know I've done a deal in Colombia! Something incredible!"

"What?"

"*Do.*"

"Two what?"

"*Do* containers."

"Tiles?"

"Are you crazy?"

"Marble?"

"Marble be blowed!"

He looked around furtively and put one finger to his nose. "Shh! Uranium. Enriched uranium: forty-five thousand kilos."

They were hilarious, Sisto Da Re's tall stories. But one day he fell in love with a gorgeous Colombian woman and showered her with jewels. He married her, and she squeezed him dry within a few months. One day she disappeared.

"Where's she gone, Sisto?"

"Oh, she's not feeling too well . . ."

It seems likely that Sisto had a child, but nobody knew for sure. He suffered from edema, his belly was all swollen, and we used to tease him: never mind, you can make another baby on your own. But apart from the baby, she'd vanished with all the jewels, just like that. Even taken the furniture. It was a fairly common occurrence in Venezuela, but anyway, nobody knew. Only old Pinton, because the apartment the lady had emptied belonged to him.

Obviously, on that occasion too Sisto tried to lie his way out of it: "I'm going back to Italy . . . My wife isn't well. She needs to have treatment over there."

We never saw him again. In Italy he was the one who fell ill. He ended up on dialysis. He ended up dying of homesickness for Venezuela. He ended up as lonely as a dog, *viejo y sin plata*.

Then there was Michel, the Frenchman. He'd fled from his home country. I think he was an OAS terrorist who had specialized in eliminating Algerian agents. He had a pilot's license, and in Venezuela he'd made good use of it. He bought himself an *avioneta*, a four-seater Piper. He used it to carry officials on the Aruba-Maracaibo-Curaçao routes for the oil companies. And occasionally something for us. He was incredibly successful. There wasn't a single other Frenchman in the whole of Maracaibo, and that in itself sparked off something in the women. He died at the age of thirty-six at Palito Blanco. Perhaps the place takes its name from the traffic light: a post with three lamps stuck into the ground halfway along a straight stretch of road two miles long. The truck in front of him braked suddenly, startled by the traffic light, and blocked his path. The driver must have been a novice. A slab of rock slid down from its precarious perch and hit Michel's car, chopped it in half, and carried away my friend's head. Sliced it clean off.

The person who found him was another of our group, Captain Leonardi, the Sicilian irredentist. They called him Romeo because of his Clark Gable mustache and his slicked-back hair, and also because of that slightly risqué hobby of his: he liked scrubbing up the black girls and then kicking them out. Very tall and dark, with a black beard, he looked like an Arab, but an Arab prince, and he had a thing about black girls. It turned him on like crazy to make them into real ladies. They all came from the *ranchitos* and had never worn a pair of shoes. He would dress them, bejewel them, make them up, and take them around with him everywhere, dressed up like Parisian models. He would put books on their heads and get them to walk—for their posture, as they say. They never lasted more than five or six months. After six months at most he'd turn up with a new one. His aim was to make money so he could return to Italy and begin the conquest of Trinacria.

Captain Carmelo Leonardi was a Sicilian independence fighter; he had been involved with Pisciotta and Giuliano. Then in 1946 he must have stuck his neck out too far and had to get out. He too was a pilot, and much in demand because engines were the only thing he was more picky about than women. He was renowned for his punctuality, and his punctuality regularly got him into trouble. In all the companies he worked for, he never lasted more than a year, because if any client turned up late he would leave him standing and take off at the pre-arranged time. In South America, *hombre!* Unbelievable. Once he flew me to Aruba: the flight plan specified takeoff at 9:10, and I had to be there at 8:30 on the dot.

"Remember, at eight thirty-five I'm shutting up shop and leaving."

And there was no persuading him. He wouldn't take you on board after that time, even if you were the Pope himself. Indeed, his real misfortune was to leave the minister for development behind on the tarmac because he was late. That guy really did get his own back.

The Honesty of the Calabrese Brothers

Now and then we were joined by three other fine Italians from the south: Cecè Calabrese and his brothers. I knew Cecè because he was the partner of a big shot in the tile business. His grandfather was from Paola and had left early in the twentieth century. A clever guy, as soon as he arrived down here, he opened a jewelry store in Maracaibo, with a Venezuelan front man for a partner, as prescribed by the local laws. Things went well, and he brought his children and grandchildren over, later leaving each of them a piece of his estate—in particular his three boys, who inherited one business each, an optician's, a foundry, and the jeweler's.

But the three Calabrese brothers didn't get on: three head-of-the-family mentalities, three suns in one sky. Too many. They were always bashing one another. The eldest, now known as "the old man," inherited the foundry and drank some liquid aluminum by accident: it went down into his esophagus and destroyed it. He lost one eye, and now, before he ate, they had to open his mouth with a stick and shove it down to open his esophagus as well. If the Calabrese brothers had an argument, their way of resolving it was to arm themselves with baseball bats and lock themselves up in a storeroom: the one left standing at the end was right. The second brother was an architect. One day he asks me to do some marble tiling in a block of three flats. The Calabreses are people who pay, so I don't raise any objections, and I give him an estimate. When it comes to signing the agreement, however, he tells me that he's not actually the owner of the apartments. The owner is his brother Cecè, the youngest. And he asks me, *"Pero, dónde está lo mío?"* But where's mine?

I turn a deaf ear; then I see what he's getting at. He has a room to refurbish himself, and he wants some marble.

"What kind of marble?"

"Siena yellow."

"Siena yellow . . ."

It's pure gold. Siena yellow is the marble of the old Florentine churches. Or, if you prefer, of Valentino's atelier in New York. The couturier made a fireplace out of it. It must have cost him as much as a basilica in Cortona. Not even someone like Versace could have afforded that particular marble.

I don't have any, but I know where to find it. Rover Marble can give me twenty square meters of Siena yellow tiles made in the Venetian fashion. "In the Venetian fashion" means a mixture of rejects and fragments polished up and stuck together with marble glue. I put this to him, and his face lights up: *"Okay. Éste es lo mío!"*

He knew what he was doing, all right, the bastard. I get the marble, send it to him, and at the same time send him the bill for the work in his brother's flats. But not a single dollar appears. So I set off to pay him a visit, with the idea of grabbing him by the lapels. Metaphorically speaking, of course. Then I think it might be a better idea to call on the jeweler: his brother Cecè, the owner of the flats.

"What about my bill for the work?" I asked.

"And what about my brother's bill?"

"What are you talking about?"

"My brother's got twenty square meters of marble that is pure gold. Where's your bill for that stuff?"

"What do you mean, 'bill'? It was a gift!"

"It was what?"

"A gift. I had to give it to him to get the work at your place . . ."

"Hmm . . . Ah. Well now . . . Wait a minute. I think we're going to have to talk to the old man. You know how it is. This is a family matter, so it'll have to be decided by all of us together . . ."

Naturally, the old man is as furious as an alligator. "You've robbed each other!" And he unleashes a series of insults that the younger brothers take like so many blows with a stick. Then the old man decrees, "I want to pay for the marble. One of us is going to have to pay. Let's make a decision."

How they make decisions you already know: they lock themselves in the storeroom; then it's out with the baseball bats.

In the morning Cecè comes around to see me again: "If you want a dead man on your conscience, it won't be a problem. We'll leave things as they are, and I'll kill my brother."

This seems a bit harsh to me. The architect's skin doesn't interest me. I suggest that we all submit to the old man's judgment. And the old man decrees again, "We Calabreses have a name here. So we're going to pay you. Here's your check. But if you want to prevent us from killing each other, you've got to give twenty square meters of Siena yellow to Cecè too. Do you agree?"

What could I do? I agreed. I didn't want a Calabrese or two on my conscience. That, however, was not to be the last quarrel between the Calabrese brothers. One day the old man and Cecè buy a Titan in partnership. A cheap little plane bought in

Miami, paid for in cash from two suitcases. Cecè had got it from a narco, and it reeked to high heaven. Of course, he hadn't noticed this and had thought only about the price, but one fine day the old man finds his house full of FBI agents on the trail of the plane. For the umpteenth time, he decides to kill his brother, but as usual they get out the baseball bats and then make up. They leave the architect out of the plane deal— evidently they didn't trust him very much anymore. Or maybe it was a kind of punishment. At any rate, they started quarreling bitterly about who was going to fly it. Obviously the old man, having only one eye (as a result of swallowing that liquid aluminum), had "bought" his pilot's license. Cecè, however, had worked hard for his. But it made no difference. Once, they invited me up for a spin in their new toy—an hour of pure terror. Those guys even came to blows in the air over who was going to hold the joystick. Every time.

It couldn't go on like that. Fortunately, there was plenty of money in the family. So one fine day the old man decides he's going to buy a microlight all his own. He pays for it, tries it out, and there, on his first flight, the motor dies under his ass. He crashes down from the height of a seven-story building and, naturally, jumps out of the wreckage practically unscathed: only a broken leg. "We're never going to manage to kill him," Cecè says to me with a smile, the light of which I can still see now: those three loved each other like nobody else. "He's a father to me," Cecè always said, meaning the old man. "He's the one who taught me honesty." And there's no doubt that they were, indeed, in their own way, completely honest. A perfect slice of Italian culture.

LESSON FOUR: The Solution

The Making of a Drug Smuggler

Here is my own story, as far as I can tell it to you. It introduces us to the least-known of the worlds that revolve around white powder: the world of the *sistemistas*, the managers of big shipments, the guys who shift immense riches, flood continents, change the planet's destiny, and then go and drink a glass of *pisco* or rum at the San José. Guys like me.

Well, I ought to begin in the traditional way, along the lines of, "You see me now, but I used to be better than this." Twenty-two years in jail never does anyone any good. I no longer have a single organ that does its job properly. Sometimes I look into the toilet bowl to make sure I haven't evacuated my *corazón* as well. Hemorrhoids as big as porcini mushrooms, and I've got a grand total of three teeth left in my mouth. But I haven't given up. I can still chew with three teeth. I found a fantastic method for *torrone* too: I suck it until it dissolves. Then, when all that's left are the hazelnuts, I spit them out and crush them with a bottle. Let's just say I haven't lost my talent for solving complex problems.

Cocaine? Me? You won't believe this: never snorted it. My passion was marijuana. I used to smoke it on the terrace in Maracaibo, looking out over the gulf with all its oil, listening to *The Dark Side of the Moon*. It was a good life. Believe me, the narco is the freest man in the world, the embodiment of Martin Luther's freedom of the poor Christian. He's free. He just rakes in money and that's it. There are no other thoughts. Or goals. Someday I'm going to write an essay: "The Importance of Cocaine to the Development of Contemporary Metaphysics."

I was enjoying the Americas, the never-ending southern Latin sunsets, the alcoholic *mezclas*, and the panoramic terraces, but I still didn't feel I'd really made my mark there. I remember a cry that exploded in my head like a flare at Copacabana, at a critical moment in my career. I was standing near the swimming pool, on the road on the side nearest the beach, where people used to have breakfast. I was with two girls. Suddenly I heard somebody on the higher terrace shout, "Italians!" I turn around and there's this guy with a camcorder trained on another guy. "Italians!" this second guy was shouting, "America is yours for the taking!" It was Beppe Grillo, filming one of those comic documentaries on the Americas he did for Italian TV. I felt as if those words were intended for me, so I thought about that blue marvel again and decided I must do something.

There was a lapis lazuli mine at Cerro Sapo, in Peru, near Huaychao. I'd tried to buy it but hadn't pulled it off. The fact is, I have a weakness for precious stones. They're the only thing I can't resist, maybe the thing that goaded me on and made me what I am. At the same time, they've ruined me. My high-speed career began with a diploma in land surveying that I was forced to take by a postwar mother who was concerned to guarantee me a minimum of dignity, some semblance of provincial normality. Which was soon betrayed. I didn't see myself spending my whole life measuring the fields around our home. I became a sales rep, tiles, and right from the start I realized that my domain wasn't big enough for me. I was able, astute, outgoing: I soon got a job selling all over Europe. I improvised the languages, relying on gestures, grimaces, glasses drunk in company. I married an elegant girl, an interior designer. It was a time of gold Rolexes, wild mink, rings set with Burmese rubies. It didn't last long. Three months after the wedding I called her one morning from Amsterdam: "I'm never coming back." I'm rather sorry now that I left her, but what the hell. Caracas, the paradise of enterprise, was waiting for me. More tiles, mountains of tiles, and a colossal market, especially in Miami, where the rich Venezuelans went to spend their cash. *"Está barato, dame dos,"* It's cheap, give me two—that's the nickname they were given by the *caraqueño* emigrants in Florida. Those were the days of easy money from oil, of the strong bolívar against the dollar. We were all distinguished men.

In Caracas I meet Morena, my other wife, a Cuban exdancer, a stunner, the ideal person to cover me while I carry on my activities. Within a few years I'm a lord: I have all the harbormasters of the Caribbean on my payroll. I offer them bribes of 50 percent of the value of the shipments to avoid customs, but then I cheat them with false invoices. I'm the king of false invoices, and I travel and travel. Sometimes I have to bargain with a policeman who's more sharp-witted and less corrupt than the others, but I always get through. I'm in love with marble, and I roam all over South America in search of quarries.

And Morena waits. Meanwhile I learn how the bribery-based system works, where its strong points and its weak points lie. I cut my teeth, and at that stage I still didn't know what I was cutting them for.

That's when I discover that lapis lazuli mine in Peru, and I glimpse a fortune. But it'll take money, a lot of it and at once. I don't have that kind of money, so I give it some thought. In the end I manage to buy a hundred-year lease—at a cost of fifty dollars plus thirty in whores—on a piece of uncultivated land in the forest on the other side of the Cerro. My plan (never put into action, but who knows . . .) was to dig a nice little tunnel through to the quarry on the other side and help myself. But I don't have that kind of money, so I think about it some more. A client of mine comes forward, says he understands dreamers and he's prepared to buy fifty containers of marble and pay cash. An enormous sum, on the nail, enough for me to rush around to see the owner of the quarry and offer him a down payment. It's not enough, but the client has been generous, and he's in a talkative mood. He turns out to be a Colombian of the Cali cartel, the most powerful drug-smuggling organization in the world. He seizes the opportunity to ask me if I'm willing to use what he calls my undeniable logistical talents to ship co-caine to Europe. It's a way of making the money I need, and besides, I owe him a favor now.

At that time cocaine is an industry: easy to produce, easy to sell, very hard to transport. That's where people like me come in. So I get down to work, I plan, I create integrated systems of transportation and delivery, an original method that guarantees the safety of the merchandise and of the employees. And the clients take an immediate liking to my work ethic: I might de-ceive the whole world, but I never cheat a supplier. Nor do I ever let myself be cheated. If the danger is the tip-off that brings down an empire, that danger is the reason for my success. I'm the one who reduces the risk.

Naturally, my first idea is to hide the merchandise in the marble. It works, but it requires special care. I manage to deliver as much as a ton of cocaine per shipment: ten million dollars gross. Details later. But what the cartel needed above all was to invent a method that didn't depend on the bribery-based system, their greatest weakness. I was the one who invented that method. It was I who discovered the philosopher's stone. Before I come to that, though, let's take a look at the *sistemista*, the person who organizes protection for big shipments and takes responsibility for transportation.

The Sistemista's Know-how

The basic problem for this kind of professional is overcoming the cartels' mistrust. If you tell them "I need two months," they tend to go crazy. They want everything at once. You, however, need time: it's a lot of work. They're impatient at first, sure. But later, if things go well, they realize that:

1. they pay only one person;
2. they run no risks from the police: the risks are all yours;
3. they don't lose a single gram of merchandise.

After the first shipments, which you'll make with them breathing down your neck, they'll be the ones running after you to ask you to work.

Now, the *sistemista's* first concern is to sell his plan. The drug producer's standard response is "I don't give a monkey's ass about your plan. I don't want to know about it." It's their way of expressing their approval. And of showing trust. It's your field of expertise, not theirs.

Important: when asking for an advance, ask only for the payment of expenses. Make sure you get your estimate right because you can't go back to a big-time narco and tell him a little problem has arisen. It's not done. Payment for the work itself is made on delivery.

The narco might say, "I have a hundred kilos; you deliver them and keep twenty." Those are pretty mean terms. Smugglers' etiquette requires that you say no: "I'll deliver ninety, I keep ten, and you pay my expenses." It's at this point, from the counteroffer, that the war, the negotiation *al brinco rabioso*, begins.

"How long do you need?"

"Three months."

"I'll give you two."

And so on.

Later, when you're more established, you can agree to fifty-fifty: you deliver half, you keep half. The price goes up because you can use the plans you devise only two or three times at most. After that the system is blown. The most serious mistake is to underestimate the investigators. They too are guys who know their trade, who adapt, understand, and don't give up. In fact, the beauty of the profession lies in that very competition with the finest cops. It's not just the money; it's getting through under their very noses every time and being able to shout your *"Coronamos!"* at the end of a shipment, when they're hot on your heels but always two steps behind.

Anyway, after the first few times you don't tell the narco about the plan anymore; he has to trust you. The risk is that otherwise he'll put the plan into effect himself, off his own bat, and ruin it for you. Besides, he's got to put trust and money into it. The cost of the merchandise is negligible to him; his only real expense is you, the transportation.

When it comes to transportation, every market has its rate. Italy is the worst destination of all, the most notorious, so you can ask up to seven thousand dollars a kilo on every shipment. Ten years ago, the best clients were in Holland. There was no need for sophisticated systems; they were all corrupt. That's why Amsterdam was the stock exchange, that's why most merchandise passed through there. Nowadays Spain is better.

There is, of course, an international stock exchange of cocaine, a market that fixes the prices. By nature or by convention, or by an intrinsic law of commerce, it's the market with the greatest amount of imports. At the time of the great solutions, when the cartels were faced with the problem of finding a more reliable method than the bribery-based system, it was Amsterdam that set the prices all over the world. We too exported mostly to Holland.

The Dutch market was also a price controller: for example, in Scandinavia the powder was much more profitable, but the continental averages for trading were decided in the Netherlands. Nowadays, Spain controls the game, mostly because that's where the main buyers, the Calabrians, prefer to have it landed. Today Madrid fixes the prices of cocaine and the exchange rate. As I say, the prices are set where the main importers are. In my day there was a guy in Amsterdam who was capable of clearing two tons a month, retail. That kind of client is highly sought after.

But there's one characteristic of the so-called legal economy that allows my colleagues who invest in Europe to make their fortunes. The Old Continent provides a formidable pool of consumers, but above all it offers great cover for money laundering because of the unparalleled fluidity of the property market and of commercial licenses. Changing the ownership of properties, shops, and restaurants is a great way of removing suspicious traces from money. Building and selling is even better. Cocaine is money. And often the institutions, whether knowingly or not, play the game too, especially when they need to legitimize themselves. "Development of the territory," they call it, and they pay our bills partly by promoting approved building projects. A real washing machine for us, a reservoir of votes for the local politician, and who gives a damn if a few acres of woodland disappear under the concrete.

Supplying rich and closely watched markets is a game of cushions and angles, like billiards. One of the main concerns is to plan the whole route, calculating what the possible alternative destinations might be should any problems be encountered along the way. So it's a matter of finding the cushions off which you can rebound the stuff into this formidable market called the European Union. That is to say, it's a matter of identifying the countries through which you can actually move the stuff. It depends on the conditions on the ground, and on who controls the territory, but also on what's fashionable at the time, and on personal inclination. I had a thing for Poland, and Stettin was the ideal entry point. Others, especially the Nigerians, preferred Albania. We worked a lot with them in the 1990s. We used to send the merchandise via Nigeria, in the bitumen carried by the tankers. You don't find many Nigerians in the jails nowadays. They've learned to be more discreet. They used to be too conspicuous, and anyway, nowadays they prefer to make money with whores rather than with powder.

The problem with the cushions, of course, is that you need to choose your partners carefully. Anyone who stands out too much puts you in danger. In my day the ideal people would have been Venezuelans, who were great entrepreneurs but not yet particularly suspicious in the eyes of the DEA. Venezuela, with its oil, hadn't yet become part of the great cocaine industry. Colombia was the most culturally advanced of the producing countries, but its entrepreneurs were well known. Until the 1990s they knew nothing about heroin. Now they produce it. It arrived together with relations with the Italian Mafia, as a means of payment: heroin for cocaine. Cocaine is currency and sometimes used as payment for itself. An example: if you intervene in a war, the best thing is to deliver fairly sophisticated weapons together with big shipments of drugs. The client is interested in the weapons, of course, but can't pay for them. It is the shifting of the drugs from wholesale to retail, given the net profit that is guaranteed by prohibition, that provides him with the cash to pay for both the weapons and the drugs he bought wholesale. Simple and ingenious: money that produces money, a system that feeds itself. It's called "triangulation." The specialists in this technique were the Kosovars, who—it seems paradoxical now—worked in harmony with their enemies, the Serbs, led by Arkan, whom they were supplying, and who in this way succeeded in circumventing the arms embargo. In the age of market revolution, this kind of thing goes on all the time.

Cocaine was valuable merchandise, though I admit that at that time Asia—like Mexico today—had an economic advantage. Heroin was even more profitable. When cocaine was no more than 13,500 dollars a kilo wholesale, heroin was fetching as much as 30,000. But—no doubt it'll seem strange to you—we all strongly disapproved of heroin. We regarded it as dirty stuff that destroyed people, whereas cocaine ennobled them. Well, maybe.

At the peak of my golden age cocaine had reached 22,000 dollars a kilo gross. Nowadays, although the price of a kilo on the clandestine market where the stuff is produced is around 1,500 to 2,500 dollars, on the European market it can fetch as much as 15,000 and, further down the distribution chain, 80,000 to 90,000 dollars, excluding the cuts. I'm talking about pure substance—an abstraction. What reaches the nostrils of the customers is cut with substances of all kinds, but it's sold at full price, so the real profit is much higher. In any case, bear in mind that when you read official figures in police reports, if they mention wholesale prices, it's just bullshit. Either they don't know them or they exaggerate them so that they can keep a slice themselves and balance the books.

Protecting the Consignment

Even with big shipments, protection is a matter of creativity and innovative solutions. How to protect the merchandise is obviously the first concern of a responsible *sistemista*. The very first systems, now relegated to history, used shoes, tables (shipped to the United States), and flowers (one of the oldest ruses, effective only in the days of the bribery-based system: everyone in the airport had to be involved). A minor stroke of genius was the cardboard used to make the boxes for the frozen prawns that were shipped north: for years those boxes traveled steeped in liquefied coca paste. And for years nobody noticed. There was a producer of asparagus who, by cutting down on the vegetables, managed to get thirty or forty grams into every tin in a false bottom smeared with grease. But he was an un-lucky man. One day a pallet fell to the ground between the unloading bays in Guayaquil harbor in Ecuador. The tins lay scattered everywhere, but nothing happened, and our man breathed a sigh of relief. Except that immediately afterward a truck came hurtling along and crushed the tins. Coca squirted out all over the place. It was ruined too, because at that point it was soaked with asparagus brine, which contaminated it. One of the most popular methods in the days of the cartels was coffee: you put the cocaine in vacuum packs that were protected in the usual way—rubber, engine grease, that kind of thing—nothing out of the ordinary. The packets were numbered so that you knew which ones to take the cocaine out of, and they were stacked in big bags on pallets. But that's expensive.

I had my own favorites. One was wood. You could transport these enormous trees from Amazonia, trunks that weigh tons. And you needed them to be big. You could get two or three hundred kilos in one trunk; you open it, dig out the cavities, close it up, and glue it back together. You keep all the bark, because afterward you glue it back on and cover up the vertical joins. The trunks are numbered and cataloged. They were filled in Brazil by a specialized and highly reliable firm. The stuff came from Colombia through the Felicidad triangle.

Glass was another specialty of mine. At one stage I got my old pal Oscar into the business.

"Oscar, would you like to go into the glass business?"

"You bet I would!"

I organize a million-dollar shipment for him. But he knows what's going on in customs, and he tells me the officials have been checking glass lately. They open the containers. What idiots! I'm completely unconcerned. They open the containers, and what do they see? Transparent sheets of glass. How do I do it? I mix the coca paste with water, put it between one sheet and the next, seal it all around with putty, then clamp it between screw-together metal frames. That way the stuff remains liquid. When it reaches its destination, you take it out and evaporate the water. From eighty kilos of this transparent sludge (okay, semitransparent, but what do you expect? Anyway, you can't see through several dozen sheets of glass one on top of the other the way you can through a window) you get sixty kilos of good stuff. So on that glass shipment I earn 560 million lire and give Oscar 240 million. The guy in charge of the retail end of things was one of his Fernandos, who kept a kilo for himself and made about 160 million, enough to build himself a new house every trip. So it suited everyone, believe you me.

Sometimes we used the pearly kind, the finest, for these payments. That stuff keeps forever. The clients take one kilo and put it away as an investment. Some Hollywood actors can afford it or, over here, one or two big, very aristocratic industrialists. Only the very few.

In any case, as far as protection is concerned, the point is that it takes imagination. You don't always put the coca in the merchandise that you transport. If you carry a box, there will almost always be someone who opens it to see what's inside. But it's rarer for them to take the box to pieces. Now imagine that you have a couple of containers full of parquet made from Ecuadorean eucalyptus—fine wood, in other words. Is the coca in the parquet? No! You put it in the end frames of the containers, in the side rails at the bottom. The containers have hollow corner posts, a trick to avoid making them too heavy. You've sawed the wood; you've prepared the coca in cubes. (Isn't it beautiful, the geometrical dance of the cakes? Sometimes I see a world made up of little cubes, disks, tips of pyramids, and cones, all dancing against a dark background, every one made of coca, every one opalescent and beautiful.) You've prepared the coca in cubes, as I was saying, so as to balance the weight properly. You have be careful when it comes to balancing the weights. They're marked on the consignment charts, so a small difference between real weight and declared weight may mean that your shipment will be checked in customs. The cost of the eucalyptus is compensated for by the 160 kilos of coca that you can fit into a single container. Fabulous. The ones that look most innocent are the "open tops," the containers covered only by tarpaulin. They have corner posts weighing 60 kilos. If you dismantle them and modify them, you can fit 240 kilos of stuff inside. Great!

You know something? While I've been telling you this, I've had a new idea. A new system that might be worth experimenting with—it could be very effective. Listen to this: Why not impregnate the tarpaulin that covers the containers with coca paste? It's not a novelty: the specialists in small shipments have been doing it for years with clothes—remember El Mocho and the couriers in Cuba? On arrival it's easy to revive the coca base in water and then recover it by evaporation. Since the precursor chemicals are readily available in the West, you do the refining on arrival and then put the merchandise on the market at whatever percentage of purity you want. The problem for people who use clothes is that the impregnated material becomes stiff, and if someone notices and checks, you've had it. But the great thing is that container tarpaulin is *supposed* to be stiff! If you think big, you actually run fewer risks than if you improvise on a small scale.

So that's it. With ideas like this it didn't take me long to become the number one *sistemista*, with the American DEA always on my tail. I worked with everybody: guerrillas, cartels, right-wing dictators, and left-wing dictators. In the end I could afford the luxury of choosing my own clients. Now I no longer did it for money but for that inebriating buzz of playing at fox and hounds. When I scored a point—when a shipment got through, that is—I used to mark the event with my shout of joy: *"Coronamos!"* People heard it in harbors all over the world without understanding what it meant. Nothing is better hidden than that which is in full view. Remember Poe's "Purloined Letter"? It gave me great satisfaction, even when they caught me—and they did that only thanks to a tip-off from one of my business associates, of course—to see the astonishment of detectives all over the world: "Who the hell is this guy?" Because my criminal record wasn't just clean. It was spotless.

Getting Through the Ports

We're interested in electric arches. That's not their proper name, but one of us must have heard the expression in some old science-fiction film, and we started using it routinely to refer to the first radioactive or thermosensitive devices that appeared in the 1990s. Nowadays they're everywhere. Even in the big freight airports. You'll find the arch at Miami, Los Angeles, Amsterdam . . . Some of these machines are very sophisticated and analyze the density of the merchandise and the percentage of liquid it contains. They're like enormous CAT scanners installed in big ports, and they scan the loads, highlighting on a screen, using different colors, the different kinds of merchandise inside the containers. Same principle as airport metal detectors, but you could get a tractor-trailer under one of these. They give a different color to each kind of substance. Alkaloid cocaine shows up on the screen a distinctive, unmistakable yellow.

Cocaine yellow.

A real headache for the *sistemista*. Luckily, the volume of traffic in a big port is monstrous—as many as nine thousand containers a day pass through Rotterdam, for example—so the electric arch is used mainly on containers and trucks belonging to firms already under suspicion, plus a certain number of shipments chosen at random. Statistics, or pure good luck, become valuable allies of the *sistemista*.

Good luck and large numbers aside, your shipments can be saved from the arch by a very subtle technique that I'll outline shortly. But first it might be useful to know how you can trick the machine.

In theory, to get the goods through the electric arch, it's sufficient to use very thin sheets of lead, impermeable to radiation. The problem is that if you use sheets of lead, a big, suspicious black mass appears on the monitor. You have to grease the palm of some customs manager, and you'd find yourself tangled up in a bribery-based system again, like in the 1980s.

Graphite is a better method. I'm not just talking about dipping the buttons of your suit in it, as El Mocho should have done. Make a note of this. When you're choosing which materials to import, always go for ones that have the same characteristics as the thing you want to hide or disguise. For example, if you're using graphite, a nice container of pencils will serve your purpose. For small quantities carbon paper is very good (though all it takes is the slightest tear, a hole, and you're in the shit—that yellow will show up).

But this is all fancy stuff, okay for small- or medium-scale traffic. When it comes to large amounts, nobody uses these tricks, because the first axiom of the drug smuggler is: never waste time. To cover your merchandise with graphite and that kind of thing, you have to build a huge homemade machine, which takes time to assemble and then to dismantle.

Yes, you work hard, but it's better to concentrate on huge shipments, not pencils, so that you can get away, for example, with no more than two shipments a year: only two, but measured in tons. A large quantity is a difficult thing to handle, but it guarantees fewer shipments, fewer problems, lower expenses, less visibility. And it optimizes the ratio between the effort you have to put in to prepare a shipment and the return. In short, far fewer risks and the right amount of work. Admittedly, if you fail, the losses are huge, but not being continually on the market is an advantage that counterbalances this danger.

For large amounts of cocaine you have to use ships—there are no other really effective means of transport. I've heard submarines are coming back into fashion, as in the days of Don Pablo, but that's a sign of weakness, not of strength, as you might think. It means someone is having to bribe everyone in sight again, and people who do that are always vulnerable—they're paper tigers.

To stuff a ship full of cocaine, you need mathematical precision, sweat, and some good luck. Marble is always a good material because it's easy to cut. The simplest option is to put one big block of marble in each shipping container. A container has a volume of five or six cubic meters, but the maximum weight is eighteen tons, and a cube of marble with a volume of five or six cubic meters would weigh far more than that. So you cut the block small enough to keep within the weight limit.

The most common method, though, is to use marble tiles packed into crates. They're easier to handle. Obviously they occupy more space and will never weigh anything like eighteen tons; tiles, even with their crates and packaging, are far lighter than solid marble. But go about it the right way and you can get eighty one-kilo packets of cocaine into each containeer. How? You put them in the tiles. The tiles are packed in crates, which are arranged in twenty-five rows. A container can hold 160 crates, each weighing 12 kilos. It's not a huge amount:

there's a limit to how many tiles you can fit into that volume. What you do is this. First you pack the cocaine into oblong bags, each measuring 20 centimeters by 20 centimeters square and 7.5 centimeters high. Now you turn to your tiles, which measure 40 centimeters by 40 centimeters by 1 centimeter thick. Take eight tiles and cut a square hole measuring 20 centimeters by 20 centimeters in the middle of each one. Next, make a pile of ten tiles like this: pile the eight tiles with holes in the middle on top of each other, and put an uncut tile at the top and bottom of the pile. Since each tile is 1 centimeter thick, there is a cavity measuring 20 centimeters by 20 centimeters by 8 centimeters, just the right size for your bag of cocaine. The ten tiles form one packet, which you're going to put into a crate. After you've cut the eight tiles, you put a bag of cocaine into the cavity, glue the pile of ten tiles together (that's important), wrap them up, and put the packet in the middle of the crate, surrounded by packets of uncut tiles. You check that the hot crates weigh exactly the same as the clean crates. And with this trick you get eighty kilos of stuff into one container. Twenty-five containers, and you have your two tons.

You have to be careful about the weight and the randomness of the checks: it's a bit like playing roulette. You can't fill all the packs of tiles in one crate, nor all the crates in one container, nor all the containers in one shipment. Let's say that if you have a good guarantee that your shipment won't be checked, you fill, on average, one receptacle in three. And that guarantee is delivery in the dark. If you don't have it, you fill far fewer and put your hope in God. That's a safe enough method, if you think He approves of people like us. Otherwise it's safer to stick to the darkness.

There are all kinds of tiles. Nowadays the most popular are those with a thickness of eight to ten milllimeters. You don't make that kind of tile out of expensive materials, because of the high cost of the waste from the manufacturing process. They're packed in crates lined with polystyrene into which you put one tile at a time, with ribs in between to stop them touching. The tiles might measure 30 centimeters by 30 centimeters, or some other standard floor measurement. If you cut the usual holes in them, you can get one-kilo packets inside. In this case too it's a long and difficult job, but you must do the filling yourself; otherwise you're exposing yourself to possible blackmail. It's okay for someone else to cut the holes; officially, you're making holes so you can plug the tiles with wood. The combination of wood and ceramic, or wood and marble, is very fashionable at the moment. A blessing for the smuggler.

A crucial characteristic of this work is the profit margin. For every dollar invested in cocaine, you make a thousand, so if you're reasonably sure that the shipment will get through and the risks of failure are small, you can afford any additional expenditure. Starting with the tiles: on arrival, you can decide whether to give the uncut tiles away, throw them into the sea, or use them to decorate a sheikh's bathroom. Usually the best method is to give away the clean loads. There's always someone willing to accept a present without asking too many questions. I preferred to give them to humanitarian associations, charities, and NGOs: to do good, in short.

Are there any rules? Yes! Work with the most expensive materials! If you choose marble, don't use a white Carrara, which is suitable for toilets: anyone would look inside that. That's the kind of stuff the Albanians use. There's Indian Galaxy, or Absolute Black. The best, the kind with golden flecks, comes from South Africa and is worth 150 to 200 euros per cubic meter. For the same price you can get Kashmir or the Brazilian Azul Macahuba. But the best, the most beautiful of all marbles, is Azul Bahía. Wonderful stuff. It can cost as much as 500 to 600 euros per cubic meter. Imagine a container with a capacity of 350 cubic meters: it'd be worth its weight in gold even without any filling. It's the kind of thing used by Donald Trump, in Italy by Berlusconi, or by the Arabs. Who'd be so crazy as to think it had been filled with something else? They don't look at it; they contemplate it. Seriously, in the ports there are plenty of people who claim to be connoisseurs. They come to admire your Bahía marble! What a laugh. It's a gambling table where you bet on the obvious. If you come along with white Carrara or other junk suitable for apartment buildings, such as Sardinian gray or Murphy cream, it's a completely different story. Good marble works when you make a "sandwich": you split the blocks in half and put the stuff all packed together in the middle. Or, better still, you fill slabs of marble that have already been cut. The slabs are transported on special pallets. The pallet has a base and four stanchions that press the slabs of marble together (six 2-centimeter slabs for floors or 3-centimeter slabs for stairs, or smoothed ones like those used for kitchen countertops). The slabs measure 1.8 meters by 4 meters. You cut them in the middle, making a hole 25 centimeters long by 5 by 5 centimeters. You leave the two outer slabs untouched and press them all together. And you can get fifty kilos of coca inside. The same technique as with the tiles, but on a larger scale.

The real problem is that anyone who imports marble from Colombia is crazy. It's like saying to customs, "Here I am! Smash everything up until you find it, and arrest me!"

So you have to make sure no one checks. And that's possible only if the stuff travels in shipments of big-name firms, world famous and above suspicion. That is the darkness. There was a company in Argentina at that time called Zanon, the biggest ceramic tile firm on the continent, based in Neuquén. It prospered until the crash of 2001, when old Zanon, a ruthless Friulian merry-go-round operator, was kicked out and the factory was taken over by a workers' cooperative. Zanon's tiles were imported by Marazzi, a well-known tile brand in Europe, perfect for darkness. No one at Zanon or Marazzi ever knew, ever even suspected, that we were using their name! We shipped from Chile, which, as I've already mentioned, was the country least scrutinized by the DEA. We could afford to be choosy because of the profit margin. My friend, who risked bringing the coca overland by truck to Antofagasta from Bolivia, or from any other place in South America, got a thousand dollars for every kilo he transported: an astronomical profit for him, a trivial expense for us.

The money's welcome, of course, but the best part of it is making fools of police forces all over the world. They chase after you like a pack of hounds, and you hear them panting behind you, but you always keep just two steps ahead.

Nobody Looks Inside Granite

You might think about granite instead. Carrying cocaine inside granite might seem technically impossible. It's extremely hard. It takes ages to cut a hole into it, it splinters, and what's more, you can see the joints, which are impossible to camouflage (whereas with marble it's very easy). It also costs a fortune. Granite, the real thing, is one hell of an expensive material. You'll see, one day someone will come up with the idea of using gold to transport cocaine.

There's a little machine, however, that—open, sesame!— reveals the secret granite road to you. It's sold quite openly all over the world. A Hilti drill. It's designed for taking core samples from rock, and it's hand-operated. Hand-operated! It has a hollow shaft and bit through which you extract the sample. Of course, the motor is more suited for the use it's normally put to, not for boring the hardest stone in existence. But it doesn't take much to adapt it. Have you ever souped up a motor scooter? No? Well, in South America it's easy to find someone who knows how to soup up a Vespa—or anything else, for that matter. There are two simple things you need to do with your Hilti: first, boost the motor from two to four horsepower, and then extend the shaft by one meter (the original length is 67 centimeters). You need exactly 1.67 meters. Remember that. The end of the bit is made of pure diamond; it's used for boring into concrete, pipes, and things like that.

Since anything can be bought if you have cash—and if you have cocaine, you have plenty—buy yourself a nice confidential relationship with a quarry: a bribe, a party, a few whores, and you're home and dry. And you ask your confidential quarry to prepare the granite. The blocks measure two cubic meters, on average. Let's say you have ten blocks prepared, which might measure 3.8 meters by 1.3 meters by 1.6 meters in height. Oblongs. Of the ten, five you work on and five you don't.

In each of the blocks earmarked for drilling, you make six holes. Scattered, not symmetrical. It takes three or four hours. It's quite a tough job, and it has to be done well. But you extract six perfect cores, nice straight ones. At this point you need pistons. Car pistons, with the same diameter. Their internal diameters must be the same as the external diameters of the cores you've extracted. You use them as molds to make cylindrical cakes of coca paste, weighing one kilo each. Easy: all you have to do is push the stuff in with a twenty-ton press. This produces a series of big medallions measuring 15 centimeters in diameter, 5 centimeters thick. You slip seven or eight into each hole in the granite. It's best to leave a bit of play, and anyway, as well as the coca you'll have to put some little balls of lead into the cylindrical chambers that you've created, to even out the weight: coca is lighter than granite. This little ruse gets you forty, maybe even fifty kilos of powder into one block of granite. Two hundred kilos in five blocks. And so on.

One block, at a thousand dollars per cubic meter, costs you about 7,000 or 8,000 dollars. You can buy twenty blocks for 120,000 dollars. If you pay cash, you're bound to get a discount. This too is a sustainable expense.

The problem is filling up the holes you made with the Hilti. Listen, you've already thought about this. With the Hilti you have a bit with a diameter of 15 centimeters, but when you bore down, you create a little dust, and the hole will be almost exactly 15.8 centimeters in diameter. If you use the same core to make the plugs, the gap will be too wide: the plug will have some give and the joint will be even more visible. That's why you need the virgin blocks! Be honest with me, had you guessed that? I bet you hadn't. Well, now you take the blocks you didn't drill into. In one of these you make some more holes, but with a different bit. You use a 16-centimeter bit and the plug comes out perfect. What you need is a little disk about 15.8 centimeters in diameter and 15 centimeters long.

Now you pulverize some granite, mix it with putty, and push it in to serve as filler. The joint is almost invisible.

The next task is to eliminate the "almost."

Pay attention, this is important. Each block has its own serial number, spray-painted directly onto the stone. A little phrase such as BLOCCO 15 GNT ITALIA. You've already guessed, haven't you? You spray the serial number over the stoppers. This way, even the small round joint that remains on the surface is covered by the paint: AC24, right over the plug.

It's a horrible job, but it's worth the effort. I call this system the strongbox, it's so secure. There's another strongbox system too, which is less laborious and in a way even more perfect. You ask the quarry to make you six enormous blocks, measuring, say, four cubic meters, twice the average size. It's an unusual request, but the quarrymen are bound to be pleased. It's less work. And the cash payment that you guarantee makes you a valued customer. You split the blocks in half, carve out quite a large hollow chamber, fill it up, and close it by putting the two halves together and preparing the joints carefully. In this way the strongbox will be perfect. The problem is its instability. The crack might reveal itself during transportation; it might widen because of the weight of the two halves. The advantage of this over the first strongbox, the one with the holes, is that you can work in the open air. I'll explain. Drilling into granite is a nasty job that can sometimes take days. Sometimes you have to start all over again simply because the joint didn't come out well or you made a mistake with the paint. You need two campesinos: in my part of the world, you can always find as many as you want. They're ignorant and immoral. Give them two whores and a bit of money, and they won't ask any questions. You can tell them, as I used to, that you're making flagpole bases for the United Nations: the holes made with the Hilti are for putting the poles into. They swallow your story. Of course, you have to do the work yourself. It's all right for them to make the holes for you, but you'll have to make the plugs, cover them up, and clean them yourself. With the "perfect" strongbox, on the other hand, all you need to do is present them with a design for a fountain, two beautiful matching basins made of granite, and you can even have the hollow chamber made by a specialized firm. That has its advantages, but I still think the method using cylindrical holes is better: being able to cover the cracks convincingly is more important than being able to contract out the work.

I recommend something else too: don't pack away the blocks that you want to transport to Europe. Leave them out in the open, bare, conspicuous. If they're inside containers, someone might be tempted to take a look, but if they're completely visible, with their neat little serial numbers on public view, you can be sure nobody will bother. You can afford to do it because granite isn't affected in the least by atmospheric conditions and can withstand even long journeys during which it's exposed to the elements.

Once delivery has taken place, you grind the granite down into chips. You can sell it, or you can give it away as filling for abandoned quarries, for example; that way you'll be doing your bit for the environment.

Now let's do a few sums. You spend about 100,000 dollars on granite, plus the expenses of transportation within South America, which are about 20,000 dollars. With all the expenses on ships, labor, unforeseen hitches, and transportation, the most it's going to cost you is about 350,000 dollars.

You've been very prudent. You've filled only six blocks in every twenty to reduce the chances of a filled block being discovered if there's a check. You've transported 240 kilos of cocaine (a paltry amount). At a sale price of 20,000 dollars a kilo (roughly speaking, but here too we've kept our estimate low), the narco who commissioned the shipment has a return of 4.8 million dollars. Not bad, eh? What he's invested in expenses and in logistics—what he's given to me, in other words—is peanuts.

Now, it's clear that the amount transported using such a complex system is significantly higher, so the profit margin increases considerably. The moral? I use the most valuable materials—I can afford it, and this reduces the likelihood of checks—then I ship it under the names of respectable firms, using my "delivery in the dark" method, which I'll explain in a minute. In a case like this, the person responsible for logistics—the *sistemista*—can "invoice" (verbally, of course: we never use paper) for a personal commission of 4,000 dollars on every kilo transported. So even with a load as small as 240 kilos, my return is almost a million dollars. But we like to keep our estimates low, we're modest guys, so let's assume we get a commission of just 3,000, no, maybe 3,500 dollars a kilo. It doesn't make much difference. We still earn enough money to pay all our expenses. Under this very conservative hypothesis, then, we've taken home 140,000 dollars per container gross.

If we'd wanted to do things in a really big way, we could have asked the trafficker who commissioned the shipment to pay for the cost of the granite and kept our whole fee. But given the size of the take, we've decided to cover the expenses ourselves and use part of our fee to pay for the granite. That way we keep on the right side of the producer: he's impressed not only with the quality and reliability of our service, but also with its lower cost. If the Cali cartel commissions me to organize its shipments, I'll do everything I can to keep those guys happy, especially on the first few runs.

LESSON FIVE: The Philosopher's Stone

A Cover Name

This is it. You're ready to learn about the darkness, the mental and logistical masterpiece of the systems revolution.

You've organized all your covers, taken all the precautions, invented formidable systems, spent colossal sums on materials. But there's not much you can do against the electric arch. Granite or no granite, when the time of the great arch comes, you have to trust in probabilities. In a port like Miami, thousands of containers pass through every day, and if the merchandise is spread thinly among the shipments, it's not that common for the very container you've filled to end up under the arch. But you're handling mountains of money, and on behalf of other people—dangerous people at that. The risk is too high for you to trust solely in the laws of chance. So you need other protection. And the most important form of protection is a name.

What you need is a reliable name, a respectable firm—well-known and trusted. Precisely because thousands of containers cross borders every day and the traffic of goods is continuous, those that tend to go through the arch belong to little-known or suspect companies, provenances that give cause for doubt. The art of delivery in the dark relies on this fact; it's a cynical art. It implicates people who have nothing to do with it. It's a form of vampirism: you don't suck their blood, you suck their names.

I once carried 1,200 kilos under the name of a guy who had previously served as a government minister and had been importing marble—clean marble, mind—for forty years. And I did it without his knowing anything about it. If they intercept one of your shipments, the guy whose cover you're using gets into trouble. It's possible that the cops will realize what has really happened and leave him alone, but it's also possible that they'll have their suspicions and grill him. A charge of drug smuggling can get you five or six years just like that, simply for aiding and abetting.

So delivery in the dark is a dirty trick.

But what genius . . .

The only person who knows what's going on is the guy in customs who fills in forms before passing them on to the shipping agent and the authorities. No, actually, even he doesn't know. Well, he might suspect something. But you'll have taken the precaution of giving him a little present, something that will silence an oversuspicious conscience and implant in him the worry that if something's wrong, then he too is compromised.

Keep this mental mechanism in mind because it's what we base our game on: 99 percent of people who accept a bribe find a way of convincing themselves that everything is aboveboard. A man like that doesn't want any problems, least of all with his own conscience. So he's the first to rewrite the script. All it takes is a touch of imagination, a justification that isn't really even a justification, a stifled doubt, a self-absolving explanation, and—hey, presto—a universe made for narcos. The world is full of people who later say "I didn't know" while having accepted thirty thousand euros under the counter or received merchandise free of charge. Or maybe they've had invoices paid for nonexistent shipments, or they've found that transportation costs for other business deals have miraculously been dealt with (by us), stuff like that. A favor, just a little favor, what's the big deal? I give you a container of washing machines. I pay off that little debt that's worrying you. These are things friends do for each other. Don't you ever ask yourself any questions? Not one.

These people are clean, of course they are. But they never ask themselves "Why me? Why are you giving this present to me of all people?" Okay, maybe not 99 percent, but 90 percent of these people accept everything. It's in their nature.

And meanwhile:

1. the payment is made;
2. the invoices are all in order;
3. the delivery order is already signed.

You don't pay people, you don't bribe policemen, you don't run the risk of a broken link, of someone chickening out or the whole edifice falling down. Only one person knows, only one person is paid. In fact, if you've been clever, no one else knows at all. You've brought about complete darkness, the masterpiece! And after the container leaves the port, nobody checks to see where it goes. Afterward, all you need is five hundred euros to have any alterations you've made removed by a welder. You paint it and give it away to the homeless or to some NGO that takes humanitarian aid around the world and never suspects that 360 lovely kilos of pure cocaine have traveled inside the box, which is now a reformed character doing a bit of charity work. Emptying it didn't take long. When everything is ready, the clients arrive with their special equipment. Experts. They're mafiosi, not amateurs. Mafiosi, okay, but you're a service provider, not a judge. Guys who know how to do their job. A quarter of an hour is all it takes before you howl your *"Coronamos!"* Then it'll be time for payment. On deadline. To the minute. We're the most efficient of industries. And the merchandise that we really sell is credibility. Everything must happen safely and within the prearranged time frame. If you miss an appointment, you lose credibility. If you lose credibility, you lose clients. If you lose clients, you're on your own. And if you're on your own, in the end you'll get caught. It's a law. The law is called "total quality."

Let's be quite clear: delivery in the dark is based on an almost demonic ability to infiltrate shipments of healthy, virginal companies without their knowledge, to fill containers bearing the insignia of internationally famous corporations with top-quality cocaine.

But there's also something one notch down from absolute darkness. Something more prosaic and less refined, but no less demonic. I call it "auto-darkness." I'm referring to the habit some industrialists have of reviving the balances of struggling firms with injections of cash. How do they get hold of this money? By making containers available, by allowing the merchandise to be carried and praying it isn't intercepted, or hoping that if worse comes to worst, and it *is* intercepted, they can feign ignorance. Have you seen the *Back to the Future* films? What a car, the DeLorean, eh? Amazing: it flew up into the air and moved from one historical period to another, carrying its passengers through time . . . And it was full of cocaine. Have you ever asked yourself why DeLorean disappeared overnight? Well, Mr. DeLorean decided to solve some little accounting problems he had by putting powder into the tires of the cars he transported from one side of the ocean to the other. There are plenty of people like DeLorean elsewhere. I'm not naming any names, but think about the impregnated tarpaulin that gets through unnoticed because it's not surprising that it's stiff. Then think of another stiff material. The material used to make jeans, for example. When it arrives, you soak it; the paste floats up to the surface; you dry it out and treat it with acetone. Hey, presto.

But these tactics are pretty unremarkable in the scheme of things. There's the masterpiece to consider.

Delivery in the Dark

I'll use an example. You take the wheel now, put yourself in my place. You have 1,200 kilos of Bolivian cocaine that enter Brazil along the—highly dangerous—caravan routes of the *yungas* and travel to a warehouse in São Paolo or Santos via the Pantanal. Here they find twenty or thirty blocks of marble waiting for them.

The marble is supplied by a big, reputable company that knows nothing about the use you make of it. Of course, you must already have credibility in the marble industry: you must be a client the company can deal with without having to ask themselves any questions. Okay, not everyone can become a *sistemista*. There are a few prerequisites. But given the money that's involved, the prerequisites can be bought if necessary. The important thing is to be trustworthy. I'll never tire of repeating that to you.

Let's go back to the marble producer. He supplies you with thirty blocks. You've gone to a quarry in Argentina and you've bought thirty blocks under the name of John Doe, Ltd., the company with the spotless reputation, based in Italy.

So as not to create any problems, you've paid for the merchandise in cash. Cash, the magic word that forestalls every objection. The contractor's eyes glitter, and the only question that can form in his head is: Why should I ask questions if this guy pays ready money and gives it to me at once? Everyone is crazy about cash. Mark my words, everyone.

I nearly forgot: you make a great show of haggling over the price of the blocks. The negotiation must be done the South American way. A lot of shouting, swearing, stuff to drink, pauses and raised voices, lunches, dinners, and whores. But in the end you buy. You pay well and on the nail. Is that clear? Because when they see the money, they're not just happy, they're prepared to invoice for half the real value.

And that way you have them in the palm of your hand. They've made out irregular invoices. They have no interest in talking to other people about it. No more than you do.

We've entered the world of illegality, but so far it's free from the taint of absolute evil: drugs.

Right. You have the marble invoiced to John Doe, Ltd., the irreproachable European firm, a respected colossus of the industry. You have it invoiced to them, but you order the delivery for yourself. You will be the one to wait for the merchandise at the port of Santos. In person. When the blocks arrive, with the transportation paid for in advance and in cash, you give the drivers a big tip. You can also lay on a nice party with singing and dancing and a slap-up dinner with the president of the local industrialists. If you pay, they'll all be happy to dance and sit down at the table. The drivers leave again, satisfied, and the industrialists of the harbor area think you're a true gentleman and a very nice guy.

What they don't dwell on is the fact that you're the owner of thirty blocks of marble, every other one of which is going to be filled with 80 kilos of cocaine, making 1,200 kilos in all.

The costs? Let's say you paid 90,000 dollars for the thirty blocks at the quarry. Plus 500 dollars for the transportation. Plus tips. Plus the cost of having the holes made. That makes about 120,000 dollars in expenses, at a generous estimate.

You need one container per block, so the order is for thirty containers. It's a juicy, profitable order: you can be sure the carriers will be killing each other to get it. Let's calculate the expenses here too. What with transportation, loading, unloading, and whores (they always go down well with the drivers), it comes out at about 50,000 dollars. So we're up to 170,000 dollars in expenses.

They bring you the blocks, and you have in your hand the sales invoices made out to John Doe, Ltd.—the well-known international firm, etc.—and in addition to the invoices, the delivery notes for the transportation.

Your work requires you to travel. Your next stop is at the customs office in the port of arrival. Shall we say Genoa? Okay. Now you're in Genoa and you're asking at the customs office, "How much do I have to pay for this shipment?" They make out your bill, you add the taxes, add the money for the customs agency that handles the files, and pay immediately.

Pin back your ears. This is where the real game starts.

There's a guy who may suspect something irregular is going on. He's a customs officer to whom at some stage you've spun a little tale that I'll tell you about in a minute, which is the key to everything. And who, if you've been prudent, has received a present from you. And therefore has no interest in talking about it or in asking himself any questions. To take an example: John Doe, Ltd., is a firm on a par with the very biggest, like Fiat, and imports huge amounts of marble or aluminum casts weighing 650 kilos. Fiat, for example, will have 150 to 200 customs agents in every port to file their paperwork. Firms like this are perfect for the darkness. The bolder you are, the safer you are; the higher you aim, the better you work. Who would dream of checking materials bound for Fiat? And how many subsidiary firms and more or less unfathomable containers does a large firm have at its disposal for imports?

So what do you do? In Venezuela, you make out the invoices to John Doe, Ltd. (or Fiat); then you fly over to Italy, go to see the customs agents, and spin them a little tale: "Look, we tried to sell this stuff to John Doe, Ltd. (or Fiat). They didn't want it. Only I did something stupid, and now I'm in trouble. I sent the merchandise from South America before completing the order. What a fool I am! I was sure of the deal and didn't want to waste any time. And now I stand to lose money. Would you do me a favor? Make out the documents anyway. I'll buy the merchandise myself. You hand it over to me. There's ten percent in it for you." Do you see the idea? You've got to be convincing. "I was naïve. I made out the invoice and sent the merchandise, but Fiat (or rather, John Doe, Ltd.) withdrew their order, and now I've got a shipment under way, with all the expenses. Of course I don't want to lose a client like Fiat (or rather, John Doe, Ltd.). I'm not going to kick up a fuss with them. I'll solve this problem myself. Look, I've got another buyer. I'll take the merchandise back. Will you make out the papers for me with a ten percent commission? I'll leave you a deposit. As soon as the container arrives, deliver it to warehouse X."

"I'll buy it": that's the magic formula.

The agent at the customs office will give you the Fiat (I mean John Doe, Ltd.) invoices. Do you understand the dirty trick you're playing on John Doe, Ltd., or Fiat?

Of course, you've arrived in Genoa before the shipment gets there. Pay attention. The timing is important, and you must be there before the containers so that you can get yourself organized. At the Genoa customs office they've checked, and they've told you, "Yes, the shipment is due on the eighteenth. Where are the blocks going?"

"Look," you've replied, "this is the original invoice. But we've already sold the blocks. To another big firm." Do you get it? The blocks mustn't go to the warehouses of Fiat or John Doe, Ltd., which are clean. And they have to stay clean; otherwise, what kind of darkness is it? Our contaminated blocks must stay out of their way. At this point you show them the sale invoices. "Here they are. Listen, can you arrange transportation for me?" It's a service they'll readily provide in a harbor. It doesn't arouse suspicions (you happily trust others because you have nothing to hide, at least that's what they think), and all you have to do is pay. And you do pay. Immediately. That's essential. As always. "I'll call you as soon as it arrives," they reply.

Finally the stuff reaches Italy, it comes off the ships, and the trucks arrive. You contact the firm to which you assigned the transportation. "I have a problem," you say. "My warehouse is full. We'll put them in the other depot." You've prepared a depot of your own, not far away—one or two miles at most. You give them a tip and have the consignment unloaded at the warehouse that you've chosen. The crane lifts the containers off, and the trucks drive away.

You haven't got much time now. You move fast. You open the containers, take out the blocks, bring in some more trucks, and carry the blocks somewhere else. You leave the containers there, where the official unloading took place. You get the shipping agent to take them back.

You have fifteen clean blocks. Those you sell to anyone you like. The fifteen dodgy ones you empty (quickly: the mafiosi are at work) and get rid of them. For example, you've dug a swimming pool, you dump them in it, cover them up, and smooth it all over. Or you crush them into gravel, which you sell to a quarry. That kind of thing.

Everyone you've spoken to has seen only one person.

The only person that's running any risk is you.

That's the darkness, the essence of drug smuggling, the ultimate solution. Using reputable firms, maintaining good relationships (as a big importer) with the customs officers. Everyone's happy.

The most vulnerable link in the chain is the customs agent of dubious morals. But a good *sistemista* can cover himself to some extent. If you want to be safer, make friends with a *prestamista*, one of those loan sharks who sets up business near the casinos, lending money to desperate gamblers. You're a narco, remember! A king of cash, of the *brinco rabioso*—that is, a generous person, the kind of guy who pays up in full on the spot, pulls it straight out of his pockets.

Anyone who gambles in the casino sooner or later ends up broke. If he's an employee and not a millionaire, it'll be sooner rather than later. You give your first present to the *prestamista* as a reward for letting you know as soon as possible if there are any customs agents among his clients. There are, there are. When you get the tip-off, you make friends with the gambling customs man and make sure to help him out. He'll feel a bit

guilty, a bit involved. When you ask him to do you a favor—
nothing suspicious-looking, of course—he'll ask himself fewer
questions than he would anyone else.

Unless a tip-off comes from inside the system, no one will
catch you, no one will find anything. Italy works like that: the
police rely entirely on blah-blah, they have no infiltrators in the
organizations. The DEA are more dangerous and take more
risks. They lose an agent a day in Mexico and Colombia, but
even they never break a delivery in the dark without a tip-off. It
has to be a solitary job. You can't afford too many partners; you
have to do most of the work yourself. You must even do your
own accounts.

Let's do them.

You've spent 170,000 dollars.

But since you're a rogue, only about 45,000 dollars of that
appears on your receipts. You can give your friend in customs
about 20 percent of the official amount. Let's say 8,000 dollars.
Then maybe you have to carry your merchandise from Genoa
to Milan, so deduct another thousand for transportation. All in
all, however hard you try, you won't manage to spend more than
200,000 dollars.

But you've brought in 1,200 kilos of cocaine! Wholesale,
that'll sell at 23,000 dollars a kilo. Shall we say 20,000, to be
pessimistic? That comes to 25 million dollars. If you're a good
sistemista, you should get 3,500 dollars a kilo. But let's be really
mean with ourselves. We're anxious to keep our clients: let's
ask for 3,000. You've still made more than 3.7 million dollars.
Net profit, 3.5 million. Paid on delivery. Milan, did we say? You
leave Viale Testi with 3.5 million dollars in your pocket.

Wow, you're not even out on the ring road yet, and already
you feel like a king . . .

Another Hot Cargo: Money

I've made it sound easy, but driving around the ring road with three and a half million dollars isn't exactly child's play. To get the money through, there's some work involved. You don't really think payments are still made through hidden transactions, bank transfers, Chinese boxes, and virtual movements, do you? That's a myth put about by the anti-Mafia commission. It probably helps to get a few hardworking policemen the occasional paid holiday on the Cayman Islands under the pretense of making financial inquiries. No. Hidden transactions are not particularly safe. In fact, electronic money is more traceable than real money—more dangerous, if anyone really sets out to investigate.

Actually, you'd be surprised how rarely anyone investigates money at all.

But the fact remains that if you move money around with a keyboard, you're too exposed. No real trafficker would ever accept payment in anything but cash. But cash is physically cumbersome, it's bulky. My pay fills several big suitcases. The pay of one of my clients fills entire crates. Cash too is stuff that needs to be protected, stuff that can be intercepted and land you in trouble. Often the geniuses of the antidrug agencies wonder how the money gets to its destination; they invoke supranational banking laws and things like that, when all they really need to do is sniff around the ships. It's a beautiful game, getting the money through: it passes under their noses practically without any packaging, but because they're looking for packaging instead of concentrating on the money, they don't see it. In reality, moving money around is the easiest thing in the world. Some tricks are so banal I'm almost ashamed to describe them. You'll be disappointed.

On the money front there are two problems: transporting it safely, and justifying it. You may think it strange, but the second problem—technically "laundering"—is the less challenging one. Not in the sense that it isn't essential. If you don't justify money, if you can't prove where it came from, it's difficult to use. Money must always be clean, but that's not enough. However clean it may be, it's always traceable when it passes through banks or holding companies. But the methods of money laundering are numerous and very well known: any lawyer, banker, or notary could recommend one to you any day of the week. In South America it's even easier than elsewhere. The important thing is to keep the money moving around—not to be afraid to splash some of it around in tips and bribes, to err on the generous side in your payments, invest, amortize. The method we use most frequently is the revaluation of real estate, especially land. In South America there's enough for everyone: jungle, mountains, as much llano and *sertão* as you want. For example, you buy 25,000 acres of nothing on Pico El Águila, an inaccessible area of scrubland. You buy them for a thousand dollars. Then, with a bribe of another thousand dollars, you get the land valued at 30,000 dollars, and bingo, you hold the key to justifying the money you'll send to save the banks of Florida. Then I sell my land on Pico El Águila back to myself, through a front man, a friend, ostensibly for 100,000 dollars, but more likely for the same thousand dollars that I'd invested at the outset, and so, after deducting the bribe, I have 99,000 little angels as clean as springwater ready to fatten some Miami banker. All I need is a notary to certify the buying and selling. That's the point of investor credibility, something you can easily build up in any country in South America. I can assure you, illegal payment always evades detection down there.

The other problem is *moving* money, in the physical sense.

Large sums are paid in cash, and in no other way. Of course, cash is suspicious: nowadays everything else is paid for in other ways. So the payment for a shipment is made in banknotes, and the money must go to its destination, to the supplier. This is another job that you'll have to do yourself. The money travels hidden, like cocaine. If you get caught, you're in trouble. And it takes up a lot of space. It's big, bulky. Four hundred thousand dollars in wads of no more than twenty bills will fill four suit-cases—imagine what twenty million looks like. So the first precaution is to change all the money into the highest denominations possible. Forget the movies where blackmailers ask for small denominations; they're fit only for mice. In my day the best notes were the Dutch 1,000 florin and the German 1,000 mark: a million lire in a single banknote, we used to say. Nowadays the 500-euro note is a godsend. So it's very useful to have a friend in the bank who's prepared to change considerable sums into that kind of paper money for you. Not a manager—the guy you have to control is an ordinary cashier.

You vacuum-pack the banknotes, like coffee. Using a compressor, you wrap them in cellophane and suck out all the air. It seems incredible, but the volume shrinks to less than a quarter of its original size.

You have to keep on good terms with the freight companies, the respectable ones. The big ones, on which you do a kind of homeward darkness, using money instead of cocaine. Clean firms, brands that have a profile at least as high as that of Gondrand, or Levitrans. They don't know what they're carrying, and nobody checks up on them.

You can put the money in washing machines—inside the drum—or in a container of Whirlpool fridges whose inner walls are made of molded plastic. That leaves a gap of four centimeters, before the steel. You make the wads of banknotes three centimeters thick. Vacuum-packed. Some pallet loads of tiles are covered with shrink-wrap: the shipping agents run a heat gun over it; the plastic contracts and grips the pallet. There are twenty-four pallets per container. In this case too you gamble on the probabilities: you take two pallets, strip off the shrink-wrap, open two crates, put in the dollars, and that's it. With this system you can get a billion old lire into one container of tiles. Here too the expenses are marginal. In my day I would buy a container of tiles in Sassuolo worth 12,000 euros, plus 1,500 for the transportation; then I'd fill it with a billion.

Less protection is needed because money has no smell, and even under the arches the paper can look like packaging. In any case, the money doesn't go through the arch. Why? Because the shipments that are monitored are the inbound ones in Europe, not the outbound ones, and certainly not the inbound ones in South America. They're looking for drugs, not money. The money travels from Europe to South America undisturbed, in crisp, tangible banknotes. They think we all go to the Cayman Islands or to some other tax haven; they try to trace dispatches of money from Europe; they scratch their heads in front of computer screens, hack into the databases of holding companies all over the world, and put a plainclothes agent next to every bank counter in the Cayman Islands. Then we arrive on the Cayman Islands in person, carrying a suitcase full of cash laundered using the Pico El Águila trick. We arrive from Maracaibo, suntanned, smiling, suitcase in hand; we stroll past the agent, bid him good morning, say excuse me, and he smiles back, makes way for us, and we're at the counter.

Once again the key is to pay *al brinco rabioso*, in cash, immediately. Let's make a rough estimate. We buy cocaine at thirty dollars a gram. Ten or fifteen million fixes get sold every day in the United States alone. All payment is in cash: retail and wholesale, nobody accepts nonmaterial forms of payment. Let's be honest: the only people in the world who have cash are drug smugglers. Maybe arms dealers too. We're the only ones who have fresh banknotes, lots of them, always. Our merchandise is the only kind that, whatever the quantity, demands paper money and doesn't accept credit. Without paper money there would be no criminal underworld. The real phantom money is the great reserves of liquidity that circulate around the world. We're the ones who keep the luxury sector going: 80 percent of the money that lands in the pockets of Versace or Dolce and Gabbana originates with us in one way or another. Then it goes its own way, of course, and everyone has a clear conscience. The luxury industry finances the progressive newspapers with their publicity stunts, and the progressive newspapers romanticize the heroes of the War on Drugs and are so obliging as to create a glossy image of the world that is ultimately compatible with both the purchase of luxury products and a clear conscience. Everyone's happy, and the money circulates, forgetting its unhappy origins.

Of course, the illegal money produced by weapons and cocaine isn't used just by the narcos. It travels around the world paying for the dirtiest kinds of business. But also the cleanest. The totalitarianism of capital. I love it.

Daring Escape and Endgame

We work on behalf of the big cartels, organizations that have no problem paying; they have all the money they need, in ready cash. What they need is one person to solve all the problems without having to involve drill operators, customs officers, and the like. A *sistemista*. A guy who may at some point come to think he's omnipotent. That's when you're in danger of falling, and when you fall, you land with a crash, especially if, like me, you'd won the trust of the biggest players and could afford to lose two tons of cocaine with barely a shrug of the shoulders if it came to it.

I did fall.

I was sitting in my Spanish refuge. I had my headquarters in Madrid, on the Gran Vía, between the Telefónica and the Holiday Inn. I had chosen a little place right above the Café Colombia. It was an amusing network of topographical allusions. I was organizing a two-thousand-kilo shipment for a big client in South America. By now the "stock exchange" was definitely shifting from Amsterdam to Madrid because of the organizational skill of the Calabrians and Neapolitans who work in Spain on a large scale. I had set up the logistics using an unusual system: marble was constantly checked during this period, which made it practically unusable. And so I came up with the electric cable method. A magnificent darkness under cover of the biggest company of them all. I bought these big reels of cable with a copper core, and patiently, I blew in the paste using a flit pump—you know the kind I mean?—those little insecticide spray guns. I squirted it in by hand, lots of the stuff. It was hard work, but worth it. The cops still haven't solved the puzzle. The paste collected around the copper core inside the rubber tube, and I covered the cables on the outside with a spiral of insulating tape, a real rubber armor. Naturally, I left a few yards at the two ends without any filling. In that space I pumped in liquid rubber instead of coca, creating a strip of strong, clean cable in the hope that if there was a check at customs, they would cut one end of the cable only to find that it was clean.

What I hadn't reckoned with—or maybe I had, but I was

obliged to gamble anyway—was my partner's tipping them off. They were waiting for me and my cables and knew exactly what was inside them, though one detail my partner didn't know about caused them some difficulty. When they seized the shipment, the customs men found themselves up against the problem of getting the paste out without ruining it. It seemed impossible. The only way, they thought, was to cut the cable into slices, but the rubber was so strong and the paste so compressed that they had to make tiny little slices and then practically pull it out with their fingernails. It would have taken them years. But if they'd chosen to heat the rubber to liquefy it, they would have destroyed the powder too. They ended up throwing away the cables without trying the most obvious thing: pulling on the copper wire. Drawing it out. The fact is that in the center of the cable, on the copper core, I had fixed hooks facing the ends of the tube. If they had extracted the wire, the hooks would have pulled out a lovely, long white snake of coca. They didn't get it.

But they got me. When I came to Italy for a shipment, I always liked to spend a few days in my family's home village, up in the Veneto. All the people there were friends of mine, and great cocaine sniffers, so I was quite a celebrity up there. While I was waiting for the cables, I decided to spend a few days in the village. And the carabinieri of my favorite little town are still fuming over the way I slipped through their fingers in a quarter of an hour. The problem began when my Italian partner got himself caught red-handed. He, by the way, was in the bad habit of using cocaine—a mistake for anyone involved in our trade—and always had some on him. On this occasion he was carrying a kilo, which he needed for a deal of his own. A trivial amount, but enough to get you three years inside. He thinks he can't afford to take that risk. He owns luxury hotels in Padua and is married to the daughter of a high-level industrialist in a firm that makes shirts, the partner of some people in the wool business who are very well-known on both sides of the ocean. He's arrested in Rosà. A friend in the Val Sugana had asked him for a kilo, which he actually needed for another friend of his in Vicenza who in fact turned out to be a carabiniere. That's how things work where I come from. A kilo to cement friendships: it's something you never refuse. Though you should never drop your guard.

Maybe it's the Val Sugana, and the crisp mountain air, I don't know. He does drop his guard, and in three seconds flat after the delivery they have him in handcuffs. They make him a proposition straightaway: the carabinieri know how to work *al brinco rabioso* too. They must have been preparing the whole operation for some time. Maybe it was all one big trap, maybe that guy in Vicenza . . . Who knows? The fact is, the captain of the carabinieri makes it easy for him: "You tell us who gave it to you and you walk away free, without a blot on your police record."

I had a Colombian with me at the time, the grandson of a boss of the Medellín. The boss was an important man and completely above suspicion despite his provenance: a multimillionaire industrialist, a guy who owned planes, ships, whole buildings. He'd entrusted the boy to me to show him a bit of the world. Unfortunately, however, my partner, less than two hours after his capture, had already coughed up my first name, surname, patronymic, and address. We'd arranged to meet at my house, up in the village. He doesn't arrive. What's more, after I've been standing there waiting for half an hour, the street becomes crowded: ten or twelve people, male and female, all young, with mobile phones. They walk along looking at all the house numbers in the street. I'm standing right in the doorway; it's impossible to slip away. Better to act indifferent when they approach.

"Do you live here?"

"Yes."

"We're looking for a Colombian . . ."

"What for?"

"We want to speak to him."

"Hmm . . ."

There were two almost identical small apartment buildings on that street.

"I think there's a foreigner in that building over there . . ."

"Thanks."

The fact is, I had stuff all over the place: sixteen kilos in the house, another eighty hidden nearby. On top of that, a container with 360 kilos was due in from Amsterdam via Lugano. As well, of course, as the electric cables coming in to Rome. I know they're not stupid. So what's their game? They ring the bell, and the caretaker says there's no Colombian living there. They must be eighty, ninety yards, less than a hundred, away from my door. There's no room for any diversionary maneuver. And indeed the guys come back and, deadpan as gamblers, say to me, "No sign of any foreigners there."

I maintain the same nonchalant tone of voice and say, "Ask in there, then—the travel agency. Maybe they know."

Antonella, the girl in the agency, is quick on the uptake and answers their question. "Ah, yes . . . A guy with a slightly swarthy complexion . . . He comes and goes . . ."

Then they come back to me. I'm beginning to understand: they haven't got a warrant. They're spinning their web.

"Look, do you know him or not?"

"I see him occasionally. But if I had to say . . ."

"If you see him, tell him we need to speak to him."

Just like that. Nothing else. I don't ask anything. We've all understood. It's a hand of poker. Then I walk off down the street in leisurely fashion in my lightweight suit with empty pockets, and about 350 yards down the road I see my Colombian friend looking at a shopwindow in Piazza delle Erbe. I have time to hiss, "Run for it. There are carabinieri all over the place looking for you."

But he had no intention of going anywhere. He had got involved with a well-known local woman who was in the process of getting divorced from her lawyer husband.

"We've got to get out of here!" I insist.

But in fact, getting out of there wasn't a good move either. I had the container coming in from Amsterdam: 360 kilos, a routine delivery for me, but hereabouts a record seizure, the kind that makes your career. That's why the carabinieri were sticking so close to the trail. They'd been dealt three of a kind, and they were going for a full house. Maybe they thought I was more stupid than I am: it's always useful to seem a bit thicker than you are. And especially a bit thicker than the person you're talking to. Precisely because I'm not stupid, I had a thought fixed in my head. It was this: Shit, I'm ruined. It's clear that there's no way out of this mess. The only reason you're still strolling about is that they're allowing you to; all around it's barbed wire and electric shocks if you take one step off the path they've marked out. There were still phone boxes in those days, thank goodness. I go into one and immediately call my elderly friend in Colombia.

"Send somebody at once to get the container . . ."

"But what about the rest?"

"Don't worry. Sixteen kilos are definitely lost, but I'll get the rest out."

The fact is, I take pride in my work, even when I'm in the

shit. In the meantime, the carabinieri had already cordoned off the whole village and had caught the boy. Of course, it wasn't him they were really after. I find one of the guys who had been asking questions in my street standing in front of me. Grim-faced, he says to me, "Have you seen him?"

"Yes, a moment ago. Over there."

I see them running like in the cartoons. God knows why they're putting on this performance. Do they really think I think I can get away? What a game . . . I jump into my car and drive to Castelfranco to see a trusted friend. Then we come back in his car. I'd stored two oxygen cylinders in a small garage at the Hotel Belvedere, 150 yards from where the sleuths were searching. Lined with lead, of course. The garages were rented out, and all the Ferraris in the village were kept there. I paid cash, as usual, so I was welcome. My little cylinders were exactly a hundred yards from the carabinieri's barracks. That was where I had put the eighty kilos.

I return home. My wife had come to Italy with me. She looks at me.

"How's it going?"

"Everything's fine."

At that precise moment my friend from Castelfranco was taking away the cylinders in exchange for the gift of one kilo: he drooled at the mere idea. Clean as a little angel, I sleep at my home. At five o'clock I wake up and go to see a lawyer friend of mine. "Beat it" is the advice. On the stairs I meet a woman I know.

"Do you know what happened at the Belvedere?" she asks.

I look curious but say nothing.

"Two coaches full of police from Padua. They surrounded the hotel and broke the padlock of your garage."

But I knew they hadn't found anything. It was completely clean. Lead prevents dispersal, so I hadn't left a trace. They'd found the garage because my partner had squealed about that too. But I still had the car belonging to the guy from Castelfranco, and maybe it was still safe; mine was parked in full view in his front garden. Now they were searching for me, though; as furious as foxhounds, they were after me now, no more games. From the piazza I see them marching in formation to my home to get my wife. What am I going to do? I can't abandon her. I go to Venice. They won't look too carefully among the tourists, I think. From there I call the lawyer (who, by the way, is a woman).

"Don't worry. Your wife has been questioned at Vicenza. She's clean. But the flat has been sealed off."

I spend the night in a small hotel in Venice with one of my scruffiest passports. I wanted to know what was going to happen to the delivery of the container from Amsterdam. It was a fairly well protected shipment: only 360 kilos, because I'd put the stuff in the side rails of the containers, not in the merchandise. As far as the electric cables in Rome were concerned, I didn't think there was any risk: not a single piece of evidence could be traced back to me. Down there I had a Colombian who was very skilled in matters concerning electric cable. I didn't know he had already been arrested at the airport. I had spent a fortune. I had bought cable-making machines in order to do the work properly, only instead of putting copper in the cables, I'd put coca in them. That takes a lot of imagination. In addition, the cables were invoiced to a colossal, whiter-than-white company owned by an Italian with a German first name and several actresses on his books. No dog has ever gone sniffing inside that gentleman's cables.

The mistake was to send a Colombian to deal with the cables. A stupid mistake. Colombian over here equals cocaine, with all due respect to Shakira, Botero, and García Márquez. So once my partner said he thought I had something coming through Rome as well, they started watching everything that arrived down there. One look at the Colombian was enough to make them cut the cables. The ends were clean, but they're no fools, and when they have a tip-off, they persist. They uncoiled the reels, and when the first air bubble appeared, they put in a probe. Out came my snow. Only a little, because of the packing. They worked for weeks to get it out so they could use it as evidence, but as I mentioned before, they lost most of it. They weren't left with much: 120 kilos. But they had me. Between my partner and the Colombian, who of course had also confessed, they were building up a charge of 1,570 kilos of cocaine against me. There had never been a seizure on that scale in Italy. And actually there wasn't on that occasion either: the charge was entirely based on witness statements. In the United States I would have got off as free as a bird on such flimsy evidence.

But it was enough in Italy, so they set a second trap for me in Rome. The Colombian waits for me in a hotel, under surveillance and silent, and I arrive as meek as a lamb to deliver myself into the arms of the police. The fact is, although they didn't know who I was, they knew I existed. When they caught me, everyone came to see me: the DEA, the FBI, the Brazilian Guardia Civil, the Venezuelan police. You can't imagine how great it feels to see all those policemen of every kind with the same expression on their faces: "Who the hell is this guy?" The great *sistemista* was a complete stranger; they didn't have a single line on him in their files. At every *"Coronamos!"* he had vanished from under their noses without leaving a trace. Until the day they caught me, I was cleaner than the Pope in his ceremonial robes. I treated them well. They were amazed at my courtesy. The fact is, I wanted to create a bit of a smoke screen because I'd decided not to give them any names, not on any account, not even that of the partner who'd sold me out. Accepting all responsibility was the only way of maintaining my credibility, though now I was going to have to maintain it in prison instead of in business. Anyway, the game was up. As soon as I arrived in Rome, they arrested me. I gave my first name and surname and even informed them that I was wanted up in the Veneto too, and they thanked me.

They made me the same, familiar proposition: "If you tell us who gives you the merchandise and who buys it, we'll set up a protection program and you'll be able to live in style."

"I'd like that. But it's all my stuff."

"Come off it."

"I swear. Paid for in cash. You've ruined me!"

A little white lie. Of course, nobody believed it. A little white lie worth twenty-two years minimum. But I saved the asses of half the world. Let's say that on the dark side I came out shining as bright as the sun . . .

One day during the trial they take me back to the Veneto for a preliminary hearing. I tell the chief detective up there, "If you let me off, I'll arrange for you to find three hundred kilos. You'll make a record seizure, and you'll be a colonel within two years."

"What about the names?"

"I'm not giving you any people. I'll only help you find the cocaine."

"I'll think about it."

And through thinking about it, he lost out twice over. He didn't get me—I was arrested in Rome and immediately said it was all my stuff—or anyone else, or the cocaine. Anyway, in the end they seized 160 kilos from me, what with one operation and another. Do you know how much they declared? Only 119.76 kilos. With the remainder they fabricate the small finds, the ones that feed the local press—"brilliant operation," personal success, a commendation, things like that. Or pay off their informers.

In Miami, however, I suffered a major financial loss, though I had the satisfaction of fooling them too. When I was arrested, the FBI in Miami, having discovered who I was, started looking for blocks of marble surprise registered in my name. And since they're clever, it didn't take them long to find them. An enormous amount: 1,200 kilos, 24 million dollars. A disaster. Except that I'd done a darkness on myself, an auto-darkness. Nobody knew who'd ordered the blocks. And in the United States you need two independent witnesses for a prosecution. They were the ones who'd slipped up this time. They were too eager: they seized the cocaine too early. They intercepted the blocks of marble on the open sea, on a ship outside U.S. territorial waters. That was the DEA's idea so that they could act ruthlessly if need be, without legal embarrassments. Those guys are as ready to shoot as the narcos if they have to. So the captain twigged in time and managed to send a message ashore, and no one turned up at the port. They didn't have the two independent witnesses they needed to charge anyone: the ship was mine, but officially I was the victim of a delivery in the dark. A business loss, but nothing more, apart from a slight feeling of guilt about the supplier. They had seized more than a ton of my stuff, it's true. But they knew as well as I did that I had a lot more, an enormous amount stashed away somewhere else. A year later the state auctioned off the blocks with the holes in them at the port of Miami. The funny thing is that they never said a word to the newspapers, because it would have come out that they'd been well and truly shafted. It was the only time I had to spend all my credit. But it was the end of the game.

I'll tell you one more story.

Epilogue

It's over. You know a lot of things very few people know. Welcome to the market. Choose your clients carefully, and you'll be on safe ground. Not everyone is a good client. The great Italian rich sniff like mad, but they're too friendly with the powerful and too concerned about their own reputations. A golden rule for the ethical narco is never to get involved with them, never to supply them . . .

And beware of judges. All my life I've known only one class of true clairvoyant: them. When they give you thirty years, you can be sure they've told your fortune accurately. Without even reading your palm. Avoid judges and avoid addiction—those are the two rules. There's still time for a story, the strange story of a man who was ruined by judges and addictions.

They called him the Painter. He came from a good family. His brother was a bank manager in Florence, his sister a surgeon—lovely woman. He lived in Corpus Christi, Texas, on the Mexican border. He was a drunk; and by trade, appropriately enough, he imported wine to the United States. Of course, he smuggled in cocaine from Mexico; it was the roaring eighties. He had a beautiful villa and a restaurant (it's a mania with us narcos: if you don't own your own restaurant, you're a nobody). He brought the stuff over on the fruit trucks, unloaded it right inside the restaurant. It's possible that he had an accomplice in high places, but this wasn't so indispensable at that time. But he had a partner—Italian like himself, indiscreet and loquacious. So loquacious that he confides in some people from the FBI. They play along, let him talk, and finally, one evening, the agents descend on the restaurant, knowing just what they're looking for, and catch the Painter with two hundred kilos. The restaurant is impounded (the fruit of illicit earnings) and very soon afterward put up for auction. Already guessed who wins the auction? That's right, the loquacious partner.

The Painter comes off a bit worse: they take him to Houston and give him twenty years. Twenty years in those parts means at least thirteen for sure, without ever putting your nose outside the cage, not even the tip of it. Afterward, maybe, parole, release on bail if you earn it. The severity of the regime is determined by the level of security that's been set for you. There are five, and the Painter gets the fourth—meager consolation. It could have been a bit worse. Still, level four is real jail.

In prison the Painter behaves himself. He does ten years without a murmur and moves down the security levels. In the end he's at Eglin: cottages for four with a patch of garden, rehabilitation work, a bar—a small federal concentration camp paradise, nothing like the state prisons, where in order to survive, you're usually forced to choose a tribe, which is decided mainly on the basis of your ethnic group. Eglin is a place well suited to a guy from a very good family like the Painter.

But he missed the wine.

However good a North American prison may be, there's no way you can get wine, real good stuff. In the Caribbean it's different. There, if you have the money, you can get burgundy brought right into your cell every week. But this was the United States.

The Painter consults his lawyer, who suggests he serve his last three years in Italy, his native country. Janet Reno was at the Department of Justice at the time; the regime was fairly lax. He thinks it over and decides he likes the idea. He gets things moving. At Eglin he studies and paints; in the cottage he has a cell to himself and his own key too. He loves Munch and reproduces *The Scream* on request. That anguished face in the midst of the acid colors is very popular among the inmates, but it's popular outside too, and outside you can sell it for 150 dollars. He does some van Goghs too, and he's not short of money now. His job is cleaning twelve yards of corridor. He keeps it spotless, the pride of the whole block. In the morning he goes to the buffet: bacon, bread hot from the oven, then the gym.

Until the day Janet Reno grants him Italy. Regina Coeli prison in Rome. Instant transfer and instant nasty surprise.

He can't believe it. Ten to fifteen people crammed together in one big room; communal toilet full of encrusted shit; smell of sweat, fear, and other things best left unnamed; no personal effects. He thinks he's going mad, and from the first day he realizes he's not going to make it. He shouts, protests, looks for someone he can tell that his contract with Janet Reno didn't stipulate these awful conditions.

He cracks up. At night he can be heard all over the block, shouting for hours things like, "Pimps! You're all a bunch of pimps! Bastards! I'm not having it! Forty square meters they promised me! I've got a right to my forty square meters, do you hear?" And so on.

What do they do? Pack him up and send him off to another prison, in Viterbo. Quieter. He calms down a little. His family sends him five hundred thousand lire a month, and he invests in cigarettes and exchanges them for wine to get over his depression. He drinks thirteen or fourteen Tetra Paks a day, revolting stuff. He sweats, stinks, his skin exudes the smell of vomit typical of cartoned prison wine. He quarrels with the warders every day. His favorite exclamation: "Spaghetti eaters! You're worse than the Mexicans!" Who knows, maybe by that time he'd convinced himself he really was a Texan. Not a day passes without him filing a complaint and getting reported himself. Like a true citizen of the empire among the savages. Any chance he'd had of getting time off for good behavior has gone now. His lawyer keeps warning him, "If you go on like this, you'll do even more than the thirteen years that were agreed on. And with no day release." But he digs in his heels. He has his mind set on his legal rights, that idiot of a narco. Making trouble has become a mania by now, and he grows increasingly prickly.

He convinces himself of one thing. They do it deliberately: they always put penniless people in his cell because they know one of the unwritten rules in there is that if your cellmate is poor, you maintain him. So the Painter yells, and always at night, if possible: "I only want people with money! There's nothing in my contract about having to maintain these fucking spaghetti eaters!" And he starts writing petitions. He even stands outside the cells of the new admissions (that's what they call them, "new admissions") and demands to see a statement of the assets and liabilities of those destined for his block.

So the years pass. And he, needless to say, doesn't get out. When the thirteenth year arrives, he's still inside. The last time he saw a landscape without bars was from the window of the plane placed at his disposal by Ms. Reno. Release comes two years late. Fifteen instead of thirteen. He asked for it, is what everyone thinks. He bids farewell to his last cellmate, a guy who, for once, he hasn't had to maintain, and gives him a Picasso, one of his own. "Now I'm going to leave"—it's his idée fixe—"and fly straight to the USA. Then Venezuela," where he knows some people he met in the Texan prisons.

He leaves.

But he stops at the first bar.

He starts by draining two bottles of wine. Then he remembers how much he used to like whiskey. He collapses right there at the bar. He wakes up in a fury, shouting. They take him to a hospital and diagnose cirrhosis. He does three or four months of detoxification, then moves to Milan and disappears.

Whenever you met him, on the streets of Milan, near the neon-lit bars on the outskirts of town, you always knew where the conversation would end: he would compare the Italian prison to the one in Mexico City where he'd once done a month because of a kilo they'd found in his car. Needless to say, Mexico always came off best. On that occasion he had called an American lawyer who sent him ten thousand dollars' bail money. But in the meantime, inside, he'd already become a little king. He had money, and he kept it in his pocket, safely, without any worries. With 150 dollars he maintained the whole block. He lived in the new part of the prison, where there was even a restaurant. In Mexico he *had* plea-bargained. The judge had asked for ten years, and the lawyer had put his hand over the Painter's and whispered, calmly, "He always does that." A knowing gesture and a direct question from the Painter: "How much do I need?"

"Twenty thousand. Ten for me and expenses, and ten for bail. But you must do two or three months anyway."

"And meanwhile?"

"Meanwhile you'll have a personal warder all to yourself, meals outside, maybe whores too . . ."

These looked like being the best three months of his life. Then a legal quibble, another five thousand dollars, and he gets out. Just like that.

It's a different matter in Italy. Sealed up in a cell for most of the time from dawn to dusk like a cockroach inside a jar, among evil-smelling tramps. They may take away my freedom, but at least I can keep my own personality, he had thought when he'd entered his first Italian jail. Wrong, you American scumbag. In U.S. prisons, as in Mexican ones, you're free to walk around all day. If you get stabbed, it's your own problem, but at least you have a life. You can decide for yourself what kind of relationship you have with the other prisoners; you create your own space, organize your own day. You're still a man: sometimes you may even do some good to others, and others may help you. There's none of that in Italy. It's not prison itself that destroys you. It's being confined to a cell for twenty hours a day. They keep me alive, okay. But they destroy me. I can't use the phone. I'm allowed only six hours' visiting time a month. Now and then a social worker comes to see me and I have to rack my brains to invent some crap about how I'm rehabilitating myself, just to keep her happy. It's called "security." Did I ask them to guarantee my security? I don't want to be secure! Man is never secure. "You belong to the Third World, you Italians," the Painter used to say on those rare occasions when the wine left some part of his tongue usable. "Mexico's far more civilized. No need to put on a front there. Strange, eh? Same Catholic culture, same basic humanism . . . But when it comes down to it . . ."

In the last few years before he died, nobody talked to him anymore. He painted *The Scream* all over the walls of the little rented room where he lived. He had it inside him, that scream. Encased in the concrete of his apartment building, a new kind of prison from which he had no hope of ever escaping, he brooded on the advanced civilization that had deceived him and brought him to Italy. He dreamed the dreams of an American. He dreamed of being in prison, even spending a lifetime in prison, but with a library, a legal adviser, a telephone, walks, visits, and an identity card.

He dreamed like an American in prison, but he was only an Italian at liberty. I saw him die. The Tavernello did for him in the end, along with the pills and the insults.

A Note About the Author

Luca Rastello is a journalist with the Italian news-paper *La Repubblica* and director of Osservatorio Balcani e Caucaso, a think tank and website that specializes in the criminal economy and international relations.